BUILT IN AMERICA

BARNS

A CLOSE-UP LOOK

A Tour of America's Iconic Architecture
Through Historic Photos and Detailed Drawings

BUILT IN AMERICA
BARNS
A CLOSE-UP LOOK

A Tour of America's Iconic Architecture
Through Historic Photos and Detailed Drawings

BY THE EDITORS AT FOX CHAPEL PUBLISHING
FOREWORD BY GREGORY D. HUBER

FOX CHAPEL
PUBLISHING

"Built In America" series trademark of Fox Chapel Publishing

Barns: A Close-Up Look is an original work, first published in 2011
by Fox Chapel Publishing Company, Inc., East Petersburg, PA.

Front cover photo courtesy of Charles Moman.
Architectural drawings and black-and-white photographs courtesy of the Historic American Building Survey and the Historic American Engineering Record, Library of Congress.
Color photographs courtesy of Charles Moman and Gettysburg Daily, gettysburgdaily.com.

ISBN: 978-1-56523-562-5

Library of Congress Cataloging-in-Publication Data

Barns : a close-up look / by the editors at Fox Chapel Publishing ; foreword by Gregory D. Huber. -- 1st ed.
    p. cm. -- (Built in America series)
Includes index.
ISBN 978-1-56523-562-5
1. Barns--United States.
NA8230.B23 2011
728'.9220973--dc22

2011004501

To learn more about the other great books from Fox Chapel Publishing, or to find a retailer near you, call toll-free 800-457-9112 or visit us at *www.FoxChapelPublishing.com*.

Note to Authors: We are always looking for talented authors to write new books. Please send a brief letter describing your idea to Acquisition Editor, 1970 Broad Street, East Petersburg, PA 17520.

Printed in China
First printing: October 2011

TO OLD
NATCHEZ TRACE

JACKSONS CAMP CH
CEM

JOHN R. TRIMM BARN

TISHIMINGO 3.5MI.

MACKEYS CREEK

3830000

QUAD UTM 16.380520.3830220

3000

1K.M.

CONTENTS

About HABS and HAER

The Historic American Building Survey (HABS) was created in 1933 in an effort to preserve and document the country's architectural history. The program's creation came at a time when preservation efforts were being undertaken across the country. It was during the same time period that the Williamsburg colonial capital was being restored and the National Park Service was working to establish historical parks and National Historic Sites.

HABS was to become a part of these early preservation efforts by continuing the work of individual architects across the country. Architects who had an interest in the past, particularly the colonial era, often took steps to preserve some of the architectural history of that time period by compiling drawings and photographs of historic structures. Without the funds or backing of a large program, however, these efforts were sporadic and often centered around the areas in which the architects lived.

Since its founding, HABS has worked to bring this architectural documentation to a national level. Formed by the American Institute of Architects, the Library of Congress, and the National Park Service, HABS collects and documents a wide range of architectural resources from across the country. In an effort to provide a complete understanding of the nation's architectural history, the HABS collection includes well-known structures designed by famous architects, along with a variety of structures that reflect the building traditions of their local communities.

The Historic American Engineering Record (HAER), established in 1969, grew out of a connection formed between HABS and the Smithsonian Institution's Museum of History and Technology (now titled the Museum of American History). HAER, formed by the National Park Service, the American Society of Civil Engineers, and the Library of Congress, became the means of documenting sites and structures that were historically important to the development of engineering and industry.

HAER is instrumental in documenting structures such as bridges, ships, steel works, railroads, and canals. While HABS focuses on documenting architectural style and design, HAER seeks to preserve an understanding of the internal workings of the machinery found within historic buildings. Most recently, this has meant a thorough documentation of maritime structures.

The preservation efforts of both HABS and HAER have allowed this book to come together as a compilation of the wealth of historic information the two programs have documented.

Since its founding, HABS has helped document architecture from the colonial period, such as the house pictured here, as well as countless other architectural styles.

FOREWORD

Most individuals, in their travels, have seen a few old barns here and there. Most can identify a barn just from its exterior aspects: they know a barn when they see one. But a look at a barn's interior traits and features has not been the experience of the great majority of people. Many know there are old beams, haylofts, and stables for farm animals that constitute much of the old structure, but beyond that, they are about as familiar with the internal construction of a barn as they are with the inner workings of a jet engine. Now that is about to change.

The book that you are now holding—*Barns: A Close-Up Look*—is a wonderful introduction to early American barn architecture. By the time you have read the last paragraph, you might not be an expert on barn construction, but you will certainly come away with much greater esteem for the way in which barns were conceived and built. You might even feel a profound gratitude knowing barn builders had to overcome numerous obstacles to build these grand monuments that served past agrarian environments. The purpose of these barns, after all, was to help provide food for growing families and a growing nation.

For many, the general lack of familiarity with architecture can be related to the dearth of information available about eighteenth- and nineteenth-century buildings. In certain cases, many of these structures have not been well documented, and, attendant to this, little or nothing has been written about them. One type of building that has, very strangely and perhaps even curiously, not been well chronicled, particularly in North America, is the vernacular barn. Until the middle of the twentieth century, historians had, for unknown reasons, simply ignored this indispensible farm building. This is particularly surprising because the barn, taken in a broad anthropological context, was absolutely critical for cultural development, given that man could not have progressed from a nomadic lifestyle to a civilization had he not developed this instrument of storage.

This lack of attention to the barn as a proper subject of study changed forever in the mid-1950s with the influential writing and artistic skills of Eric Sloane, the famed painter and author of Americana. In particular, his classic book *An Age of Barns* (1966) helped draw attention to the barn and its architectural diversity. The book contains a wide array of North American barn types, and is replete with sharp pen and ink drawings and several of Sloane's paintings. The book was the first to present such a variety of barn types in one volume.

Expanding on this topic, over the past thirty-five years, various writers have produced dozens of barn books, but only a very few of them, incidentally, have been genuinely scholarly. Most of them lack an in-depth look at the great assortment of barn types across diverse construction eras that remain in the United States. Consistently, they have lacked an adequate number of illustrations that include interior structure. One distinct exception to this is the book you are now reading.

On the title page of this book, the word "tour" appears, and that is just what you are about to experience—an expedition into an exceptional cross section of barns across the country. It is true, there are far more barn types in the United States than this book includes, but still, it renders a broad view of certain architectural expressions that at one time existed in the lexicon of barn builders' construction modes.

Despite the creativity of barn builders and the seemingly limitless potential of barn construction, after viewing and examining nearly 5,000 barn structures of varying types in many geographic areas over the past thirty-five years or so, I have come to understand that many builders actually performed their tasks, relative to particular time frames, under some rather strict constraints. They were limited by the availability of materials, to a large extent by their own experiences (barns they saw built at the time), and by the particular demands, visions, and pocketbooks of their farming customers. Builders left a great deal of evidence in the barns they erected of using their creative faculties to solve certain problems they faced.

All fourteen of the barns you will find on these pages, without exception, were conceived and constructed following these general guidelines. Whether you are considering barns of great size, like the Culp-Sweitzer barn built in the Pennsylvania style near Gettysburg, Pennsylvania, or the diminutive M. V. Riddle log barn in the great-named county of Tishomingo, Mississippi, barns were built under the specific directives of both time and place. And now, several generations after each was erected, we can revel in what the builders accomplished, recognizing, of course, that these structures were also a matter of necessity for farmers' survival. These barns are, on the most fundamental level, a record of decisions made by both builders and farmers alike at particular homesteads.

We also know that at one point, another and different type of decision was made regarding this book. The editors had to determine what barns would be included in these pages. Perhaps by some inspiration, they consistently chose wonderful barns that were exceptionally recorded and documented many years ago. All are illustrated in full measure, and, after looking at each of them in the book, there is not a shadow of doubt that every reader will come away with some understanding of the construction details and overall appearances of the barns. The reader will also learn a bit of information about each barn, such as the name of the owner, details about certain structural alterations, and how each barn functioned.

Take, for instance, the rare and very interesting John Black Jr. Barn, which stands in the Eayrestown vicinity of Burlington County, New Jersey. There are more than a dozen sizable photos and drawings of the barn that show literally hundreds of construction aspects that combine with sixteen other smaller sketches of specific details. The barn was more than amply recorded. Features of every exterior wall and most, if not all, of the framing units are exactly known. The structure includes a very rare king post or vertical beam support of the roof structure. Whether this barn actually still exists or not is in one sense immaterial. The barn was so well documented that a near duplicate of the structure could be created just from the pages of this book.

This book is illustrated to the point that this replication process could be applied to almost all of the other barns that are included. In the case of the remarkable George Hall round barn in Jackson County, Indiana, details abound on how the barn was constructed. The eye-filling drawing on page 41 by itself is almost worth the price of the book. The original thoughts that went into the framing elements of the roof structure are plainly seen. The geometric design, with no exaggeration, is almost "otherworldly." One comes away with the sense that the builders of this barn were

not playing games in the least bit, but were all business every step of the way. The barn, along with all the structures on these pages, represents a coordination of the efforts of many people. They were all precision-minded, something that is reflected in the exact construction elements of the barn and readily seen in both the photos and the drawings.

Barns: A Close-Up Look was never conceived as a comprehensive historical treatise, or even as a general guide to all barns across every state in the union. What it is, however, is a broad overview of how barns in many states were conceived and constructed. Richly illustrated books like this one come around on the barn literature scene only rarely. It is unusual to a degree that it might just serve as a model for future barn books. Even to a long-seasoned veteran of barn watching, an addition such as this book is well warranted. It has a very definite use to anyone who loves barns.

—Gregory D. Huber, Barn historian

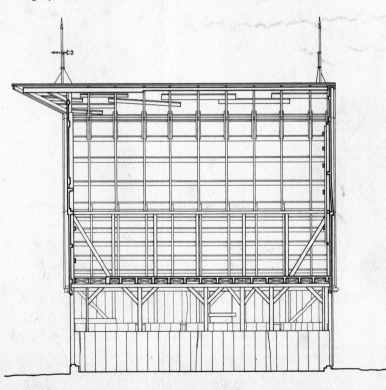

ABOUT THE AUTHOR

Gregory D. Huber is a barn and house historian, independent scholar, consultant, and principal owner of Past Perspectives and Eastern Barn Consultants—both historic and cultural resource consultation companies based in Macungie, Lehigh County, Pennsylvania. His special focus is in house and barn histories of historic homesteads in southeast Pennsylvania and beyond. A student of early vernacular architecture since March 1971, Huber has specialized in pre-1840 house and barn architecture of the Holland Dutch and Pennsylvania Swiss-German. He has documented more than 7,500 vernacular buildings, including more than 3,000 homestead houses and almost 5,000 barns in the east since the mid-1970s. He is the author of more than 140 articles on barn and house architecture and is the co-author of two books: the second edition of *The New World Dutch Barn* (2001) and *Stone Houses—Traditional Homes of Pennsylvania's Bucks County and Brandywine Valley* (2005). Huber is currently writing a major book on the architecture of vernacular barns in Pennsylvania. He was the recipient of the Alice Kenney award in 1997 and the Allen Noble Book Award in 2003, issued by the Pioneer America Society. He is available for historic house and barn consultations.

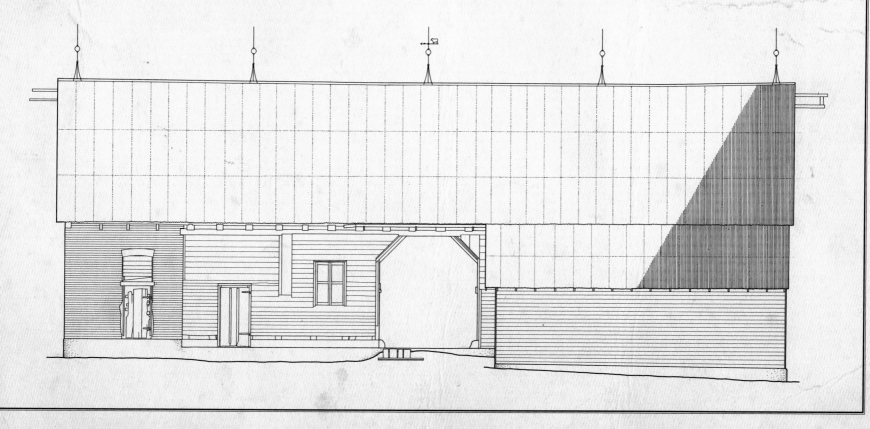

Cochran Grange Barn

New Castle County, Delaware • Built in 1834

The Cochran Grange Barn was built in 1834 using the bank barn design. The barn was built to consolidate various farm functions in one building, such as food storage, equipment storage, and animal housing. The ground floor was used for stables, while the upper level was used to store hay. An earthen ramp was built leading up to the upper floor loft on the north side of the barn, allowing wagons to access it from the outside rather than bringing supplies into the barn's ground floor and carrying them to the upper level. The barn is currently in use as a hay barn.

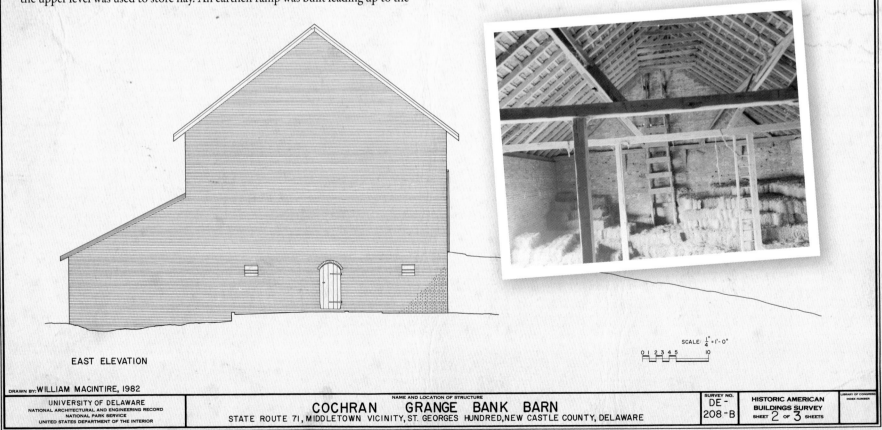

EAST ELEVATION

SCALE: $\frac{1}{4}$" = 1'-0"

0 1 2 3 4 5   10

DRAWN BY: WILLIAM MACINTIRE, 1982

UNIVERSITY OF DELAWARE
NATIONAL ARCHITECTURAL AND ENGINEERING RECORD
NATIONAL PARK SERVICE
UNITED STATES DEPARTMENT OF THE INTERIOR

NAME AND LOCATION OF STRUCTURE
COCHRAN GRANGE BANK BARN
STATE ROUTE 71, MIDDLETOWN VICINITY, ST. GEORGES HUNDRED, NEW CASTLE COUNTY, DELAWARE

SURVEY NO.
DE-208-B

HISTORIC AMERICAN
BUILDINGS SURVEY
SHEET 2 OF 3 SHEETS

LIBRARY OF CONGRESS
INDEX NUMBER

The Cochran Grange Barn is a front wall brick-arched bank barn constructed in 1834. A bank barn refers to a barn that is constructed into the side of a hill, providing access to at least two floors at the ground level.

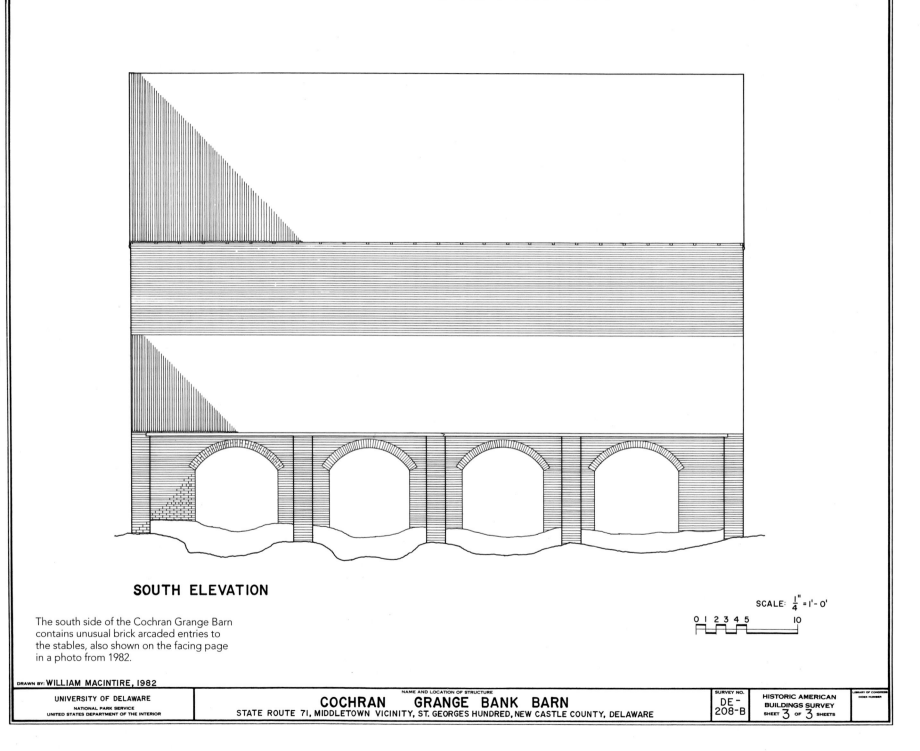

SOUTH ELEVATION

The south side of the Cochran Grange Barn contains unusual brick arcaded entries to the stables, also shown on the facing page in a photo from 1982.

SCALE: $\frac{1"}{4}$ = 1'- 0'

0 1 2 3 4 5   10

DRAWN BY: WILLIAM MACINTIRE, 1982

UNIVERSITY OF DELAWARE
NATIONAL PARK SERVICE
UNITED STATES DEPARTMENT OF THE INTERIOR

NAME AND LOCATION OF STRUCTURE

COCHRAN GRANGE BANK BARN
STATE ROUTE 71, MIDDLETOWN VICINITY, ST. GEORGES HUNDRED, NEW CASTLE COUNTY, DELAWARE

SURVEY NO.
DE-
208-B

HISTORIC AMERICAN
BUILDINGS SURVEY
SHEET 3 OF 3 SHEETS

LIBRARY OF CONGRESS
INDEX NUMBER

HABS NO. DE-208-B-7

W·S·D

80

The east wall of the runway, located on the barn's main floor, contains the drawing of a Delaware Bay oyster schooner.

This door, located on the east side of the barn, is an entryway to the ground level.

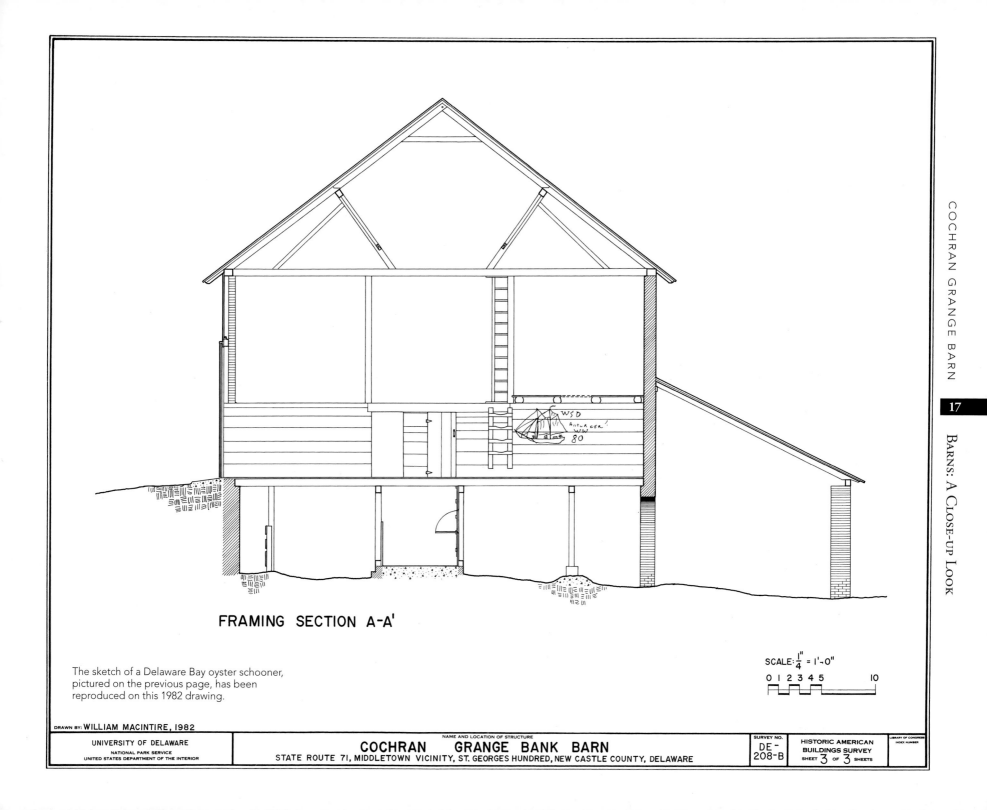

FRAMING SECTION A-A'

The sketch of a Delaware Bay oyster schooner, pictured on the previous page, has been reproduced on this 1982 drawing.

SCALE: $\frac{1"}{4}$ = 1'-0"

0 1 2 3 4 5   10

DRAWN BY: WILLIAM MACINTIRE, 1982

	NAME AND LOCATION OF STRUCTURE	SURVEY NO.		LIBRARY OF CONGRESS INDEX NUMBER
UNIVERSITY OF DELAWARE NATIONAL PARK SERVICE UNITED STATES DEPARTMENT OF THE INTERIOR	**COCHRAN GRANGE BANK BARN** STATE ROUTE 71, MIDDLETOWN VICINITY, ST. GEORGES HUNDRED, NEW CASTLE COUNTY, DELAWARE	DE- 208-B	HISTORIC AMERICAN BUILDINGS SURVEY SHEET 3 OF 3 SHEETS	

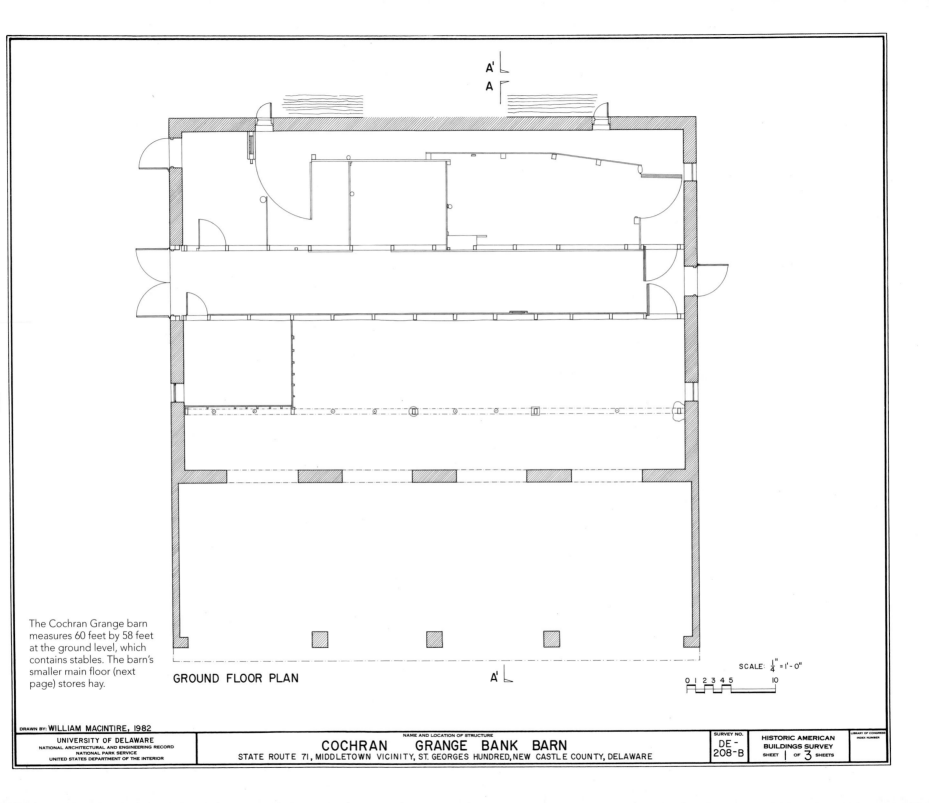

A'

A'
A

The Cochran Grange barn measures 60 feet by 58 feet at the ground level, which contains stables. The barn's smaller main floor (next page) stores hay.

GROUND FLOOR PLAN

A'

SCALE: $\frac{1}{4}$" = 1'-0"

0 1 2 3 4 5   10

DRAWN BY: WILLIAM MACINTIRE, 1982

UNIVERSITY OF DELAWARE
NATIONAL ARCHITECTURAL AND ENGINEERING RECORD
NATIONAL PARK SERVICE
UNITED STATES DEPARTMENT OF THE INTERIOR

NAME AND LOCATION OF STRUCTURE
COCHRAN GRANGE BANK BARN
STATE ROUTE 71, MIDDLETOWN VICINITY, ST. GEORGES HUNDRED, NEW CASTLE COUNTY, DELAWARE

SURVEY NO.
DE-208-B

HISTORIC AMERICAN BUILDINGS SURVEY
SHEET 1 OF 3 SHEETS

LIBRARY OF CONGRESS
INDEX NUMBER

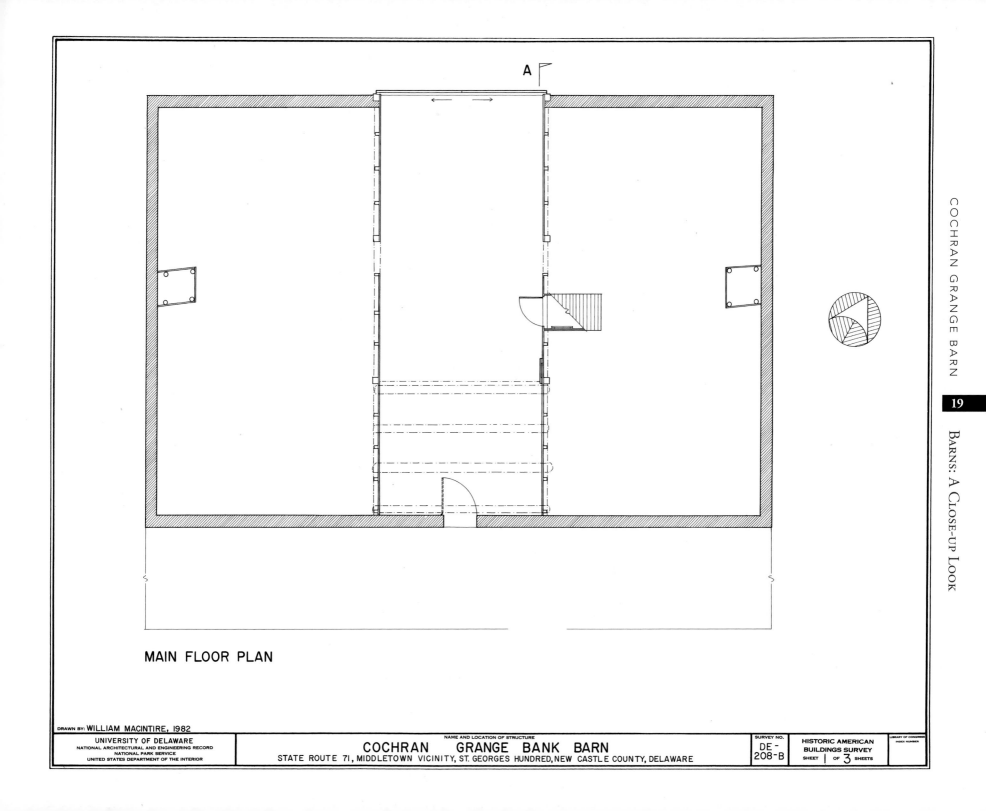

A

MAIN FLOOR PLAN

DRAWN BY: WILLIAM MACINTIRE, 1982

| UNIVERSITY OF DELAWARE
NATIONAL ARCHITECTURAL AND ENGINEERING RECORD
NATIONAL PARK SERVICE
UNITED STATES DEPARTMENT OF THE INTERIOR | NAME AND LOCATION OF STRUCTURE
COCHRAN GRANGE BANK BARN
STATE ROUTE 71, MIDDLETOWN VICINITY, ST. GEORGES HUNDRED, NEW CASTLE COUNTY, DELAWARE | SURVEY NO.
DE-
208-B | HISTORIC AMERICAN
BUILDINGS SURVEY
SHEET 1 OF 3 SHEETS | LIBRARY OF CONGRESS
INDEX NUMBER |

The barn's main floor is used for hay storage. Using an earthen ramp built along the barn's north side, wagons can access the main floor directly, eliminating the need to lift the hay from the ground floor to the main floor. Stored this way, it's easy to toss the hay down to the stables as it is needed.

Culp Farm Barn

ADAMS COUNTY, PENNSYLVANIA • BUILT CIRCA 1850

Henry Culp, owner of Culp Farm and the Culp Farm Barn, was born about 1809. By 1860, he was one of the wealthiest people in Gettysburg, owning more than $20,000 in estate funds. A hill on the Culp Farm, later named Culp's Hill, played a crucial role during the Battle of Gettysburg. At the time of the battle, Culp's Hill was the location of the Union Army's right flank. The trees growing on the hill were sparse, providing a clear view of the surrounding area and making it the perfect location to position troops. Many bloody skirmishes were waged between Union and Confederate troops as Confederate soldiers tried to win control of the hill. Henry's nephew, Confederate soldier Wesley Culp, fought in these skirmishes and died during the battle. The barn, located behind Confederate lines, was used as a field hospital for soldiers wounded in the fighting. The barn is built on a mortared stone foundation and contains a ground level and upper hayloft level, each of which was constructed with stone and wood siding. A ramp constructed on the north side of the barn allows direct access to the hayloft level.

Gettysburg Daily, www.gettysburgdaily.com

DRAWN BY: DAVID J. ANTHONE & LESLEY M. GILMORE

GETTYSBURG NATIONAL MILITARY PARK
NATIONAL PARK SERVICE 1987
UNITED STATES DEPARTMENT OF THE INTERIOR

NAME AND LOCATION OF STRUCTURE
CULP FARM—BARN
GETTYSBURG N.M.P.   GETTYSBURG VICINITY   ADAMS COUNTY PENNSYLVANIA

SURVEY NO.
PA-5379A

HISTORIC AMERICAN
BUILDINGS SURVEY
SHEET 5 OF 6 SHEETS

LIBRARY OF CONGRESS
INDEX NUMBER

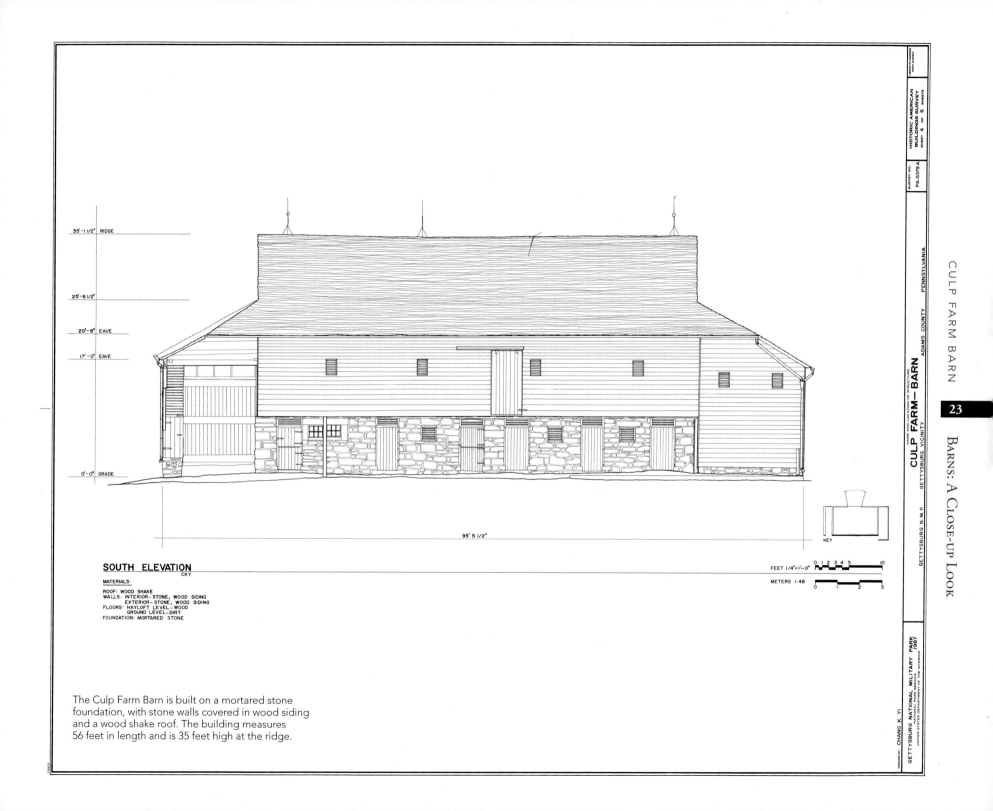

35'-11 1/2" RIDGE

25'-6 1/2"

20'-8" EAVE

17'-0" EAVE

0'-0" GRADE

95' 5 1/2"

KEY

SOUTH ELEVATION
CKY

MATERIALS:

ROOF: WOOD SHAKE
WALLS: INTERIOR– STONE, WOOD SIDING
     EXTERIOR– STONE, WOOD SIDING
FLOORS: HAYLOFT LEVEL– WOOD
    GROUND LEVEL–DIRT
FOUNDATION: MORTARED STONE

FEET 1/4"=1'-0"   0 1 2 3 4 5   10

METERS 1:48   0   1   2   3

SURVEY NO.
PA-5379 A

HISTORIC AMERICAN
BUILDINGS SURVEY
SHEET 4 OF 6 SHEETS

NAME AND LOCATION OF STRUCTURE
CULP FARM–BARN
GETTYSBURG VICINITY   ADAMS COUNTY   PENNSYLVANIA

GETTYSBURG N.M.P.

GETTYSBURG NATIONAL MILITARY PARK
NATIONAL PARK SERVICE
UNITED STATES DEPARTMENT OF THE INTERIOR
1987

DRAWN BY: CHANG K. YI

The Culp Farm Barn is built on a mortared stone foundation, with stone walls covered in wood siding and a wood shake roof. The building measures 56 feet in length and is 35 feet high at the ridge.

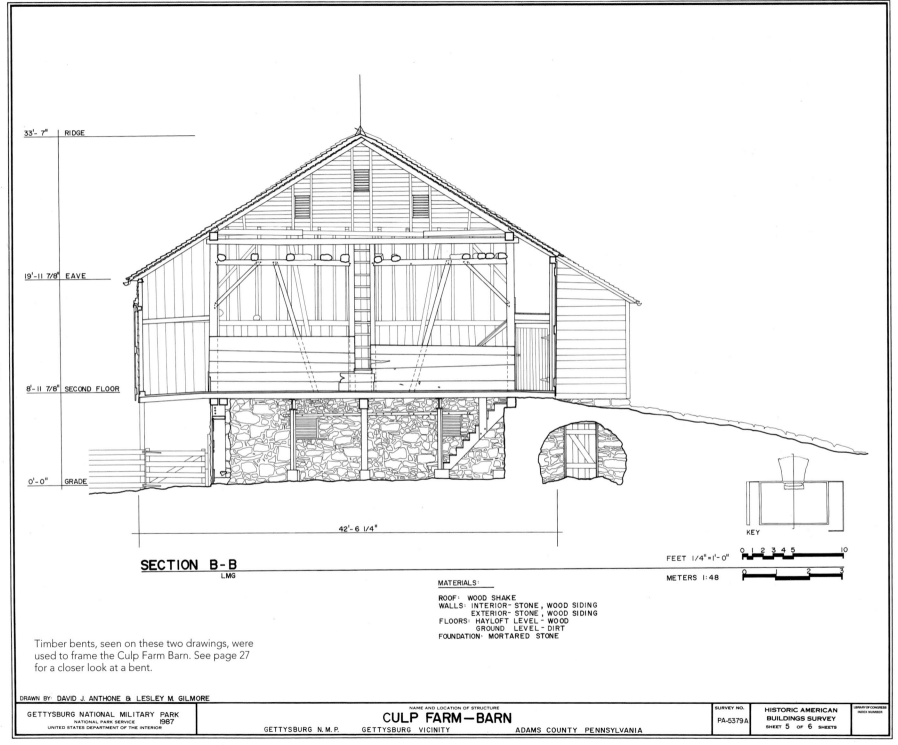

33'- 7" | RIDGE

19'-11 7/8" | EAVE

8'-11 7/8" | SECOND FLOOR

0'- 0" | GRADE

42'-6 1/4"

SECTION B-B
LMG

KEY

FEET 1/4"=1'-0"

METERS 1:48

0 1 2 3 4 5   10

0   1   2   3

MATERIALS:

ROOF: WOOD SHAKE
WALLS: INTERIOR- STONE, WOOD SIDING
        EXTERIOR- STONE, WOOD SIDING
FLOORS: HAYLOFT LEVEL- WOOD
        GROUND LEVEL- DIRT
FOUNDATION: MORTARED STONE

Timber bents, seen on these two drawings, were
used to frame the Culp Farm Barn. See page 27
for a closer look at a bent.

DRAWN BY: DAVID J. ANTHONE & LESLEY M. GILMORE

| GETTYSBURG NATIONAL MILITARY PARK NATIONAL PARK SERVICE 1987 UNITED STATES DEPARTMENT OF THE INTERIOR | NAME AND LOCATION OF STRUCTURE **CULP FARM—BARN** GETTYSBURG N.M.P.   GETTYSBURG VICINITY   ADAMS COUNTY PENNSYLVANIA | SURVEY NO. PA-5379A | HISTORIC AMERICAN BUILDINGS SURVEY SHEET 5 OF 6 SHEETS | LIBRARY OF CONGRESS INDEX NUMBER |

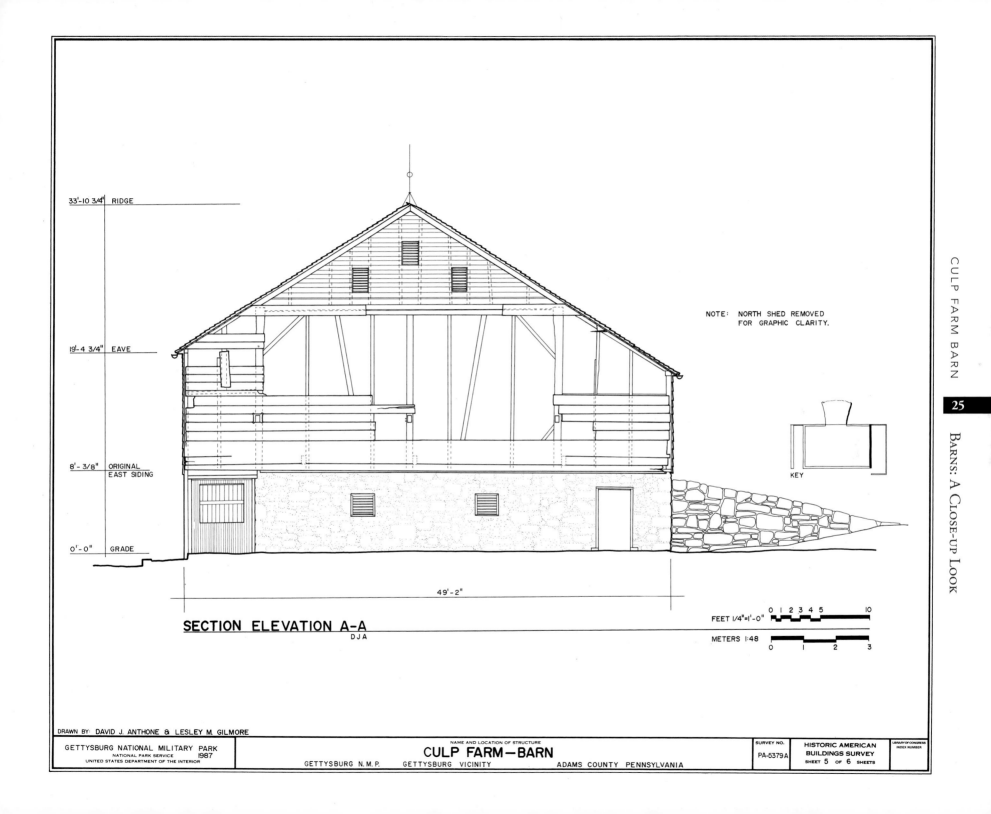

33'-10 3/4" RIDGE

NOTE: NORTH SHED REMOVED
FOR GRAPHIC CLARITY.

19'-4 3/4" EAVE

8'-3/8" ORIGINAL
EAST SIDING

KEY

0'-0" GRADE

49'-2"

SECTION ELEVATION A-A
DJA

FEET 1/4"=1'-0"   0 1 2 3 4 5   10

METERS 1:48   0   1   2   3

DRAWN BY: DAVID J. ANTHONE & LESLEY M. GILMORE

GETTYSBURG NATIONAL MILITARY PARK
NATIONAL PARK SERVICE   1987
UNITED STATES DEPARTMENT OF THE INTERIOR

NAME AND LOCATION OF STRUCTURE
CULP FARM—BARN
GETTYSBURG N.M.P.   GETTYSBURG VICINITY   ADAMS COUNTY PENNSYLVANIA

SURVEY NO.
PA-5379A

HISTORIC AMERICAN
BUILDINGS SURVEY
SHEET 5 OF 6 SHEETS

LIBRARY OF CONGRESS
INDEX NUMBER

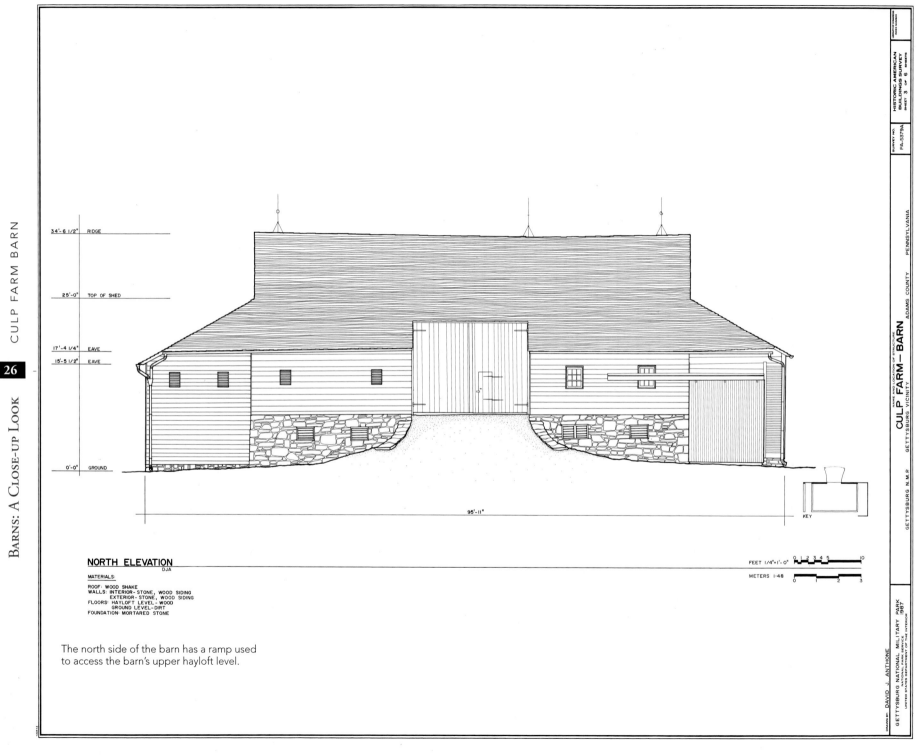

34'-6 1/2"   RIDGE

25'-0"   TOP OF SHED

17'-4 1/4"   EAVE
15'-5 1/2"   EAVE

0'-0"   GROUND

95'-11"

KEY

NORTH ELEVATION
DJA

MATERIALS:

ROOF: WOOD SHAKE
WALLS: INTERIOR - STONE, WOOD SIDING
       EXTERIOR - STONE, WOOD SIDING
FLOORS: HAYLOFT LEVEL - WOOD
        GROUND LEVEL - DIRT
FOUNDATION: MORTARED STONE

FEET 1/4"=1'-0"   0 1 2 3 4 5   10

METERS 1:48   0   1   2   3

The north side of the barn has a ramp used
to access the barn's upper hayloft level.

DRAWN BY: DAVID J. ANTHONE

GETTYSBURG NATIONAL MILITARY PARK
NATIONAL PARK SERVICE
UNITED STATES DEPARTMENT OF THE INTERIOR
1987

SURVEY NO.
PA-5379A

HISTORIC AMERICAN
BUILDINGS SURVEY
SHEET 3 OF 6 SHEETS

CULP FARM-BARN
NAME AND LOCATION OF STRUCTURE
GETTYSBURG N.M.P.   GETTYSBURG VICINITY
ADAMS COUNTY   PENNSYLVANIA

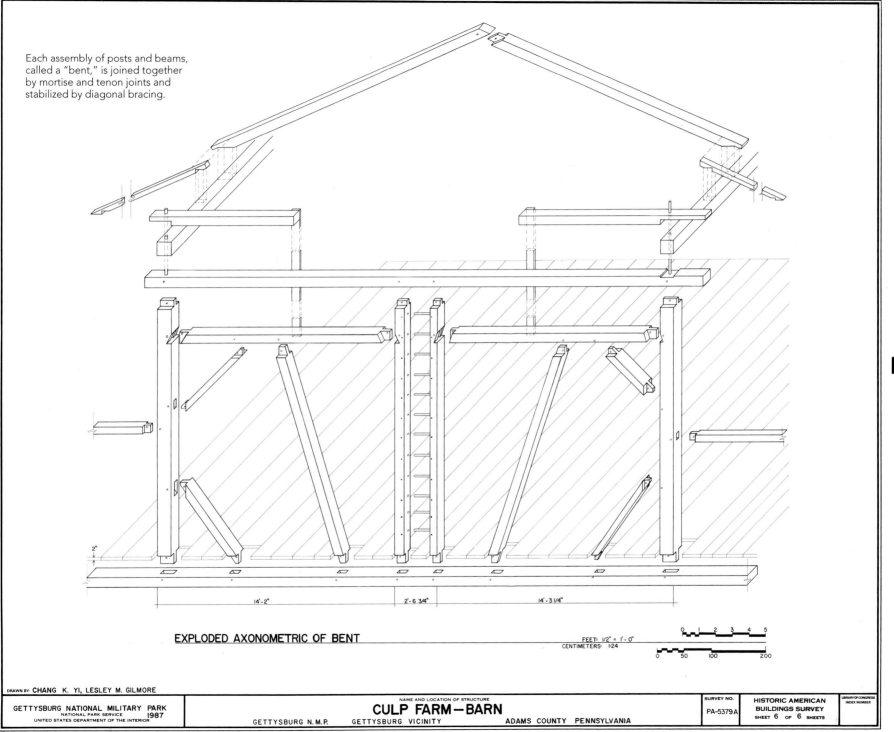

Each assembly of posts and beams, called a "bent," is joined together by mortise and tenon joints and stabilized by diagonal bracing.

14'-2" 2'-6 3/4" 14'-3 1/4"

2"

EXPLODED AXONOMETRIC OF BENT

FEET: 1/2" = 1'-0"
CENTIMETERS: 1:24

0 1 2 3 4 5

0 50 100 200

DRAWN BY: CHANG K. YI, LESLEY M. GILMORE

GETTYSBURG NATIONAL MILITARY PARK
NATIONAL PARK SERVICE 1987
UNITED STATES DEPARTMENT OF THE INTERIOR

NAME AND LOCATION OF STRUCTURE
CULP FARM—BARN
GETTYSBURG N.M.P.   GETTYSBURG VICINITY   ADAMS COUNTY   PENNSYLVANIA

SURVEY NO.
PA-5379A

HISTORIC AMERICAN
BUILDINGS SURVEY
SHEET 6 OF 6 SHEETS

LIBRARY OF CONGRESS
INDEX NUMBER

25'-6 1/2" TOP OF SHED

20'-8" EAVE

17'-0" EAVE

3'-2 1/2" FIRST FLOOR

0'-0" GRADE

42'-1"

SECTION C-C
CKY
LOOKING AT CORNCRIB

KEY

FEET 1/4" = 1'-0"
0 1 2 3 4 5   10

METERS 1:48
0   1   2   3

MATERIALS:

ROOF: WOOD SHAKE
WALLS: INTERIOR - CRIB SIDING, WOOD SIDING
      EXTERIOR - CRIB SIDING, WOOD SIDING
FLOOR: WOOD
FOUNDATION: MORTARED STONE

The barn's west-side corncrib has an overhang where wagons could unload. Corncribs were usually built with slatted walls to allow air into the crib, which would dry the corn and keep it dry until it was needed for animal feed. Today, the barn's corncrib is probably used as a shed.

DRAWN BY: CHANG K. YI, LESLEY M. GILMORE

GETTYSBURG NATIONAL MILITARY PARK
NATIONAL PARK SERVICE 1987
UNITED STATES DEPARTMENT OF THE INTERIOR

NAME AND LOCATION OF STRUCTURE
CULP FARM—BARN
GETTYSBURG N.M.P.   GETTYSBURG VICINITY   ADAMS COUNTY PENNSYLVANIA

SURVEY NO.
PA-5379A

HISTORIC AMERICAN BUILDINGS SURVEY
SHEET 6 OF 6 SHEETS

LIBRARY OF CONGRESS INDEX NUMBER

29

The Culp Farm Barn, built circa 1850, played an important role in the Battle of Gettysburg. Located behind Confederate lines during the battle, the barn was used as a field hospital for wounded Confederate soldiers.

Fountain Grove (Fountaingrove) Barn

Sonoma County, California • Built circa 1875

It is thought that the Fountain Grove Barn was built by Russian sailors hired by Thomas Lake Harris, founder of the religious colony known as the Brotherhood of the New Life. In the late 1800s, the colony took up residence at the Fountain Grove Winery, running the vineyard and conducting other agricultural endeavors in an effort to create a utopian community. In the early 1900s, Harris transferred ownership of the winery and the barn to his friend, Kenaye Nagasawa. During Nagasawa's ownership, Fountain Grove was run as a commercial vineyard and winery. After Nagasawa passed away, ownership of the barn changed frequently. The Fountain Grove Barn is a unique round structure with sixteen sides. Round barns grew to popularity in the late 1800s into the early 1900s when urbanization increased demand for fresh produce in cities, causing farming to shift to a mass-production market. Round barns were popular because they were more efficient and better suited to this production mentality. Dairy farmers in particular could take advantage of the round barn design, arranging animal stalls facing inward. Food could be stored in the center of the barn and easily distributed to the animals, while cleanup would only have to take place along the outside wall.

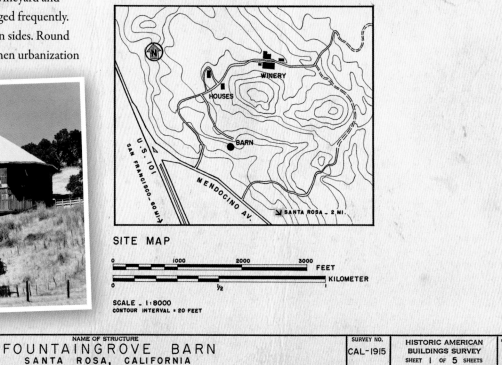

SITE MAP

SCALE - 1:8000
CONTOUR INTERVAL - 20 FEET

WESTERN OFFICE
SAN FRANCISCO, CALIFORNIA
UNDER DIRECTION OF UNITED STATES DEPARTMENT OF THE INTERIOR
NATIONAL PARK SERVICE, BRANCH OF PLANS AND DESIGN

NAME OF STRUCTURE
FOUNTAINGROVE BARN
SANTA ROSA, CALIFORNIA

SURVEY NO.
CAL-1915

HISTORIC AMERICAN
BUILDINGS SURVEY
SHEET 1 OF 5 SHEETS

LIBRARY OF CONGRESS
INDEX NUMBER

30

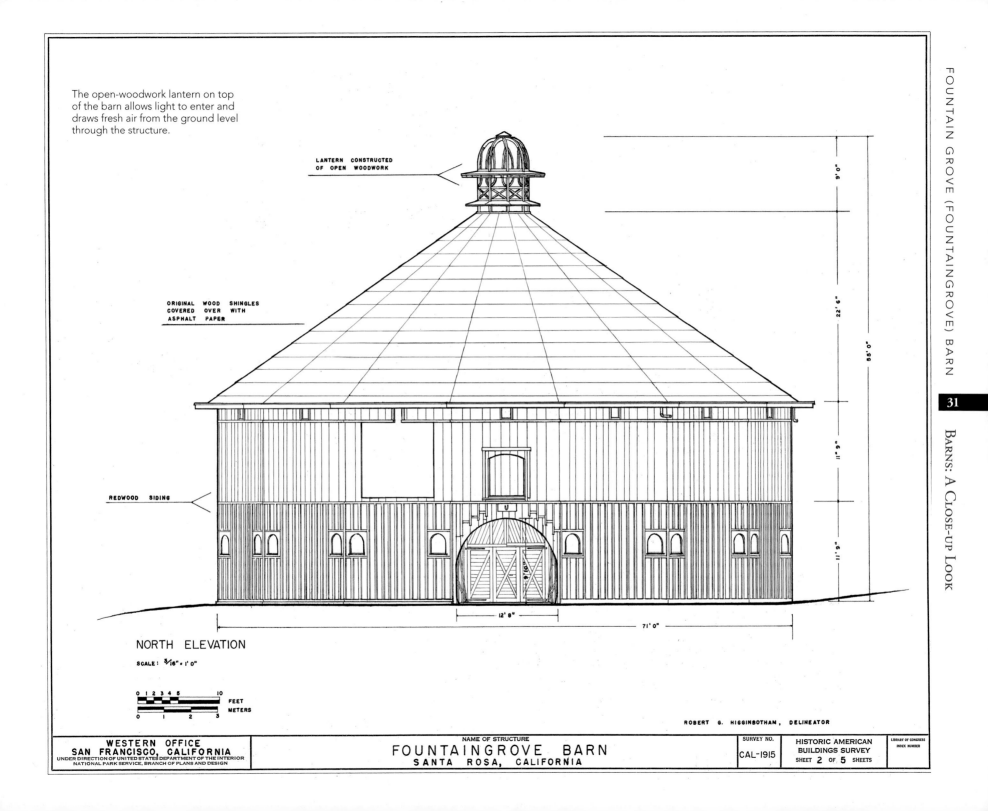

The open-woodwork lantern on top of the barn allows light to enter and draws fresh air from the ground level through the structure.

LANTERN CONSTRUCTED
OF OPEN WOODWORK

ORIGINAL WOOD SHINGLES
COVERED OVER WITH
ASPHALT PAPER

REDWOOD SIDING

9' 0"

22' 6"

55' 0"

11' 9"

11' 9"

12' 8"

71' 0"

NORTH ELEVATION

SCALE: 3/16" = 1' 0"

0 1 2 3 4 5   10   FEET
                     METERS
0   1   2   3

ROBERT G. HIGGINBOTHAM, DELINEATOR

| WESTERN OFFICE SAN FRANCISCO, CALIFORNIA
UNDER DIRECTION OF UNITED STATES DEPARTMENT OF THE INTERIOR
NATIONAL PARK SERVICE, BRANCH OF PLANS AND DESIGN | NAME OF STRUCTURE
FOUNTAINGROVE BARN
SANTA ROSA, CALIFORNIA | SURVEY NO.
CAL-1915 | HISTORIC AMERICAN BUILDINGS SURVEY
SHEET 2 OF 5 SHEETS | LIBRARY OF CONGRESS
INDEX NUMBER |

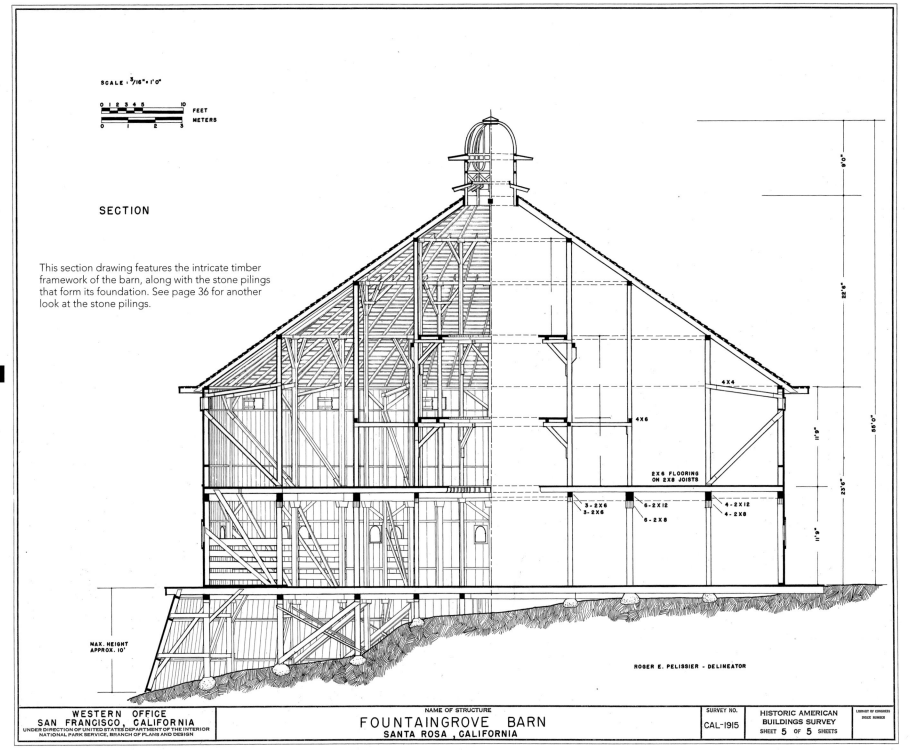

SCALE · 3/16" = 1'0"

0 1 2 3 4 5   10   FEET
                 METERS
0   1   2   3

SECTION

This section drawing features the intricate timber framework of the barn, along with the stone pilings that form its foundation. See page 36 for another look at the stone pilings.

4X4

4X6

2X6 FLOORING
ON 2X8 JOISTS

3 - 2X6
3 - 2X6

6 - 2X12
6 - 2X8

4 - 2X12
4 - 2X8

9'0"

22'6"

55'0"

11'9"

23'6"

11'9"

MAX. HEIGHT
APPROX. 10'

ROGER E. PELISSIER - DELINEATOR

WESTERN OFFICE
SAN FRANCISCO, CALIFORNIA
UNDER DIRECTION OF UNITED STATES DEPARTMENT OF THE INTERIOR
NATIONAL PARK SERVICE, BRANCH OF PLANS AND DESIGN

NAME OF STRUCTURE
FOUNTAINGROVE BARN
SANTA ROSA, CALIFORNIA

SURVEY NO.
CAL-1915

HISTORIC AMERICAN
BUILDINGS SURVEY
SHEET 5 OF 5 SHEETS

LIBRARY OF CONGRESS
INDEX NUMBER

The sixteen-sided Fountain Grove Barn is built into a hill, requiring a supporting base. The enclosed base is used as a basement.

FOUNTA
RA

The barn contains a large arched entryway on its north side, instead of the large sliding doors typically associated with barns.

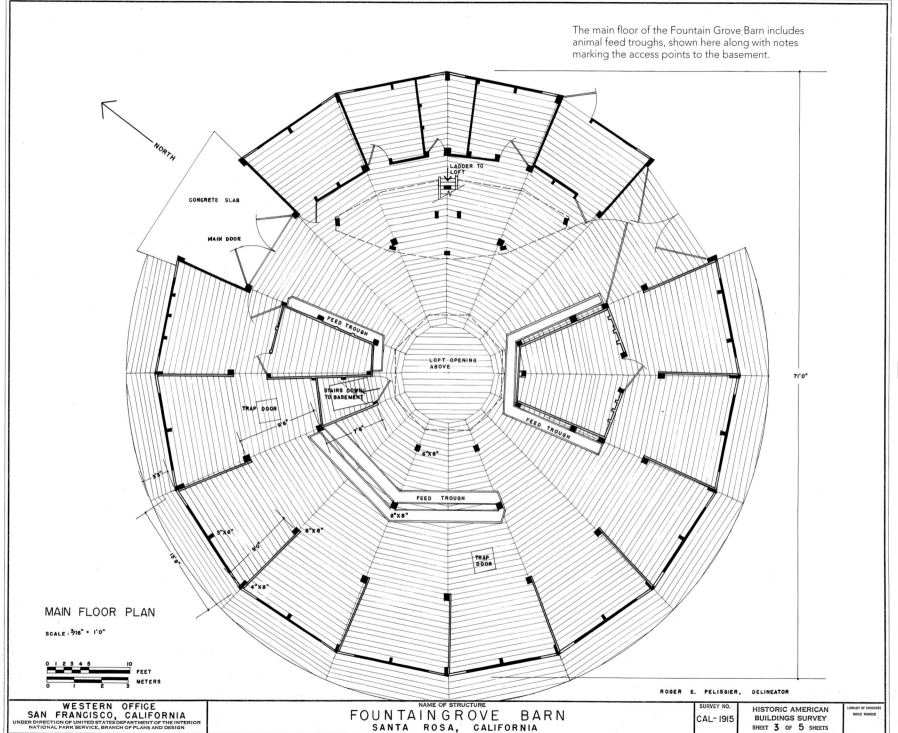

The main floor of the Fountain Grove Barn includes animal feed troughs, shown here along with notes marking the access points to the basement.

NORTH

CONCRETE SLAB

MAIN DOOR

LADDER TO LOFT

FEED TROUGH

LOFT OPENING ABOVE

FEED TROUGH

STAIRS DOWN TO BASEMENT

TRAP DOOR

9'6"

7'6"

6"X6"

5'3"

FEED TROUGH

8"X8"

13'9"

5"X6"

6"

8"X8"

4"X8"

TRAP DOOR

71'0"

MAIN FLOOR PLAN

SCALE : 3/16" = 1'0"

0 1 2 3 4 5 .... 10 FEET

0 .... 1 .... 2 .... 3 METERS

ROGER E. PELISSIER, DELINEATOR

WESTERN OFFICE
SAN FRANCISCO, CALIFORNIA
UNDER DIRECTION OF UNITED STATES DEPARTMENT OF THE INTERIOR
NATIONAL PARK SERVICE, BRANCH OF PLANS AND DESIGN

NAME OF STRUCTURE
FOUNTAINGROVE BARN
SANTA ROSA, CALIFORNIA

SURVEY NO.
CAL-1915

HISTORIC AMERICAN
BUILDINGS SURVEY
SHEET 3 OF 5 SHEETS

LIBRARY OF CONGRESS
INDEX NUMBER

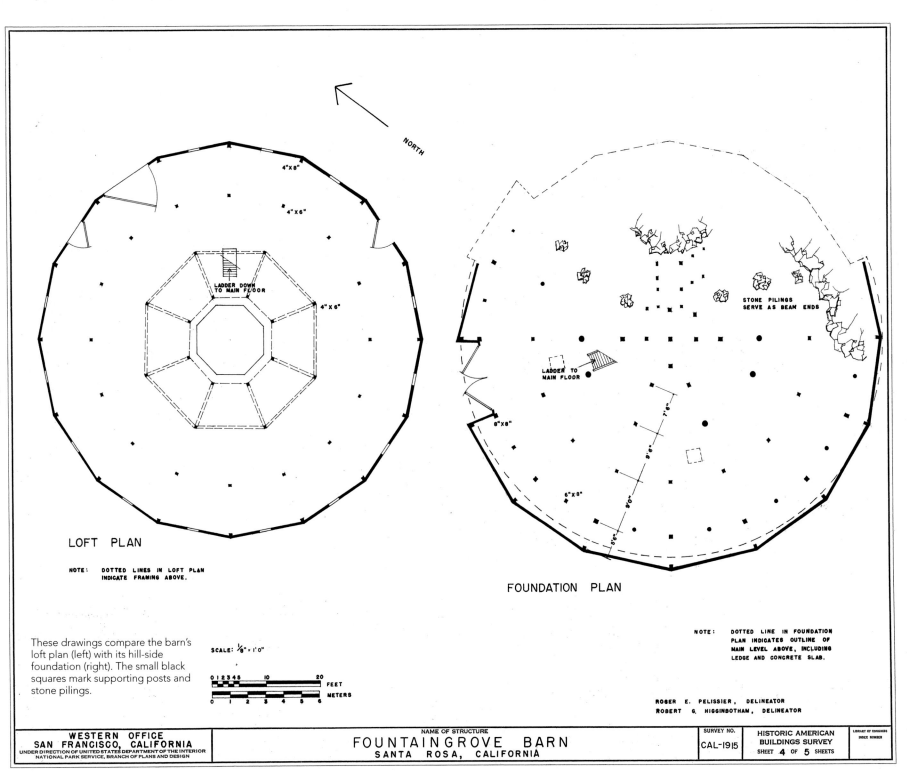

NORTH

4"X 8"

4"X 6"

LADDER DOWN
TO MAIN FLOOR

4"X 6"

LOFT PLAN

NOTE: DOTTED LINES IN LOFT PLAN
INDICATE FRAMING ABOVE.

STONE PILINGS
SERVE AS BEAM ENDS

LADDER TO
MAIN FLOOR

8"X 8"

6"X 8"

FOUNDATION PLAN

NOTE: DOTTED LINE IN FOUNDATION
PLAN INDICATES OUTLINE OF
MAIN LEVEL ABOVE, INCLUDING
LEDGE AND CONCRETE SLAB.

These drawings compare the barn's
loft plan (left) with its hill-side
foundation (right). The small black
squares mark supporting posts and
stone pilings.

SCALE: 1/8" = 1'0"

0 1 2 3 4 5   10   20
                                      FEET
                                      METERS
0   1   2   3   4   5   6

ROGER E. PELISSIER , DELINEATOR
ROBERT G. HIGGINBOTHAM , DELINEATOR

| WESTERN OFFICE SAN FRANCISCO, CALIFORNIA UNDER DIRECTION OF UNITED STATES DEPARTMENT OF THE INTERIOR NATIONAL PARK SERVICE, BRANCH OF PLANS AND DESIGN | NAME OF STRUCTURE FOUNTAINGROVE BARN SANTA ROSA, CALIFORNIA | SURVEY NO. CAL-1915 | HISTORIC AMERICAN BUILDINGS SURVEY SHEET 4 OF 5 SHEETS | LIBRARY OF CONGRESS INDEX NUMBER |

Ladders give access to the barn's hayloft from its main floor.

GEORGE HALL BARN

JACKSON COUNTY, INDIANA • BUILT DURING THE 1900S

Little is known about the history of the George Hall Barn; most of the information about the structure refers to its design. The George Hall barn is a "true circular" round barn constructed using a design that was typical of barns built during the 1900s in Indiana. Unlike many barns throughout the country, the George Hall barn seems to have been well maintained. With the exception of the barn windows, all the barn's original structural elements remain intact, including its large sliding doors. The barn was used as a shelter for cattle and for food storage and remains standing today.

38

Charles Moman

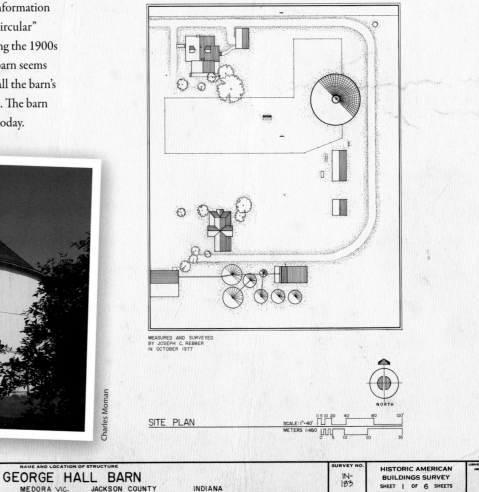

MEASURED AND SURVEYED
BY JOSEPH C. REBBER
IN OCTOBER 1977

NORTH

SITE PLAN

SCALE: 1"=40'
METERS 1:480

DRAWN BY: JOSEPH C. REBBER, 1979
BALL STATE UNIVERSITY
COLLEGE OF ARCHITECTURE AND PLANNING
OFFICE OF ARCHEOLOGY AND HISTORIC PRESERVATION
UNDER DIRECTION OF THE NATIONAL PARK SERVICE.
UNITED STATES DEPARTMENT OF THE INTERIOR

NAME AND LOCATION OF STRUCTURE
GEORGE HALL BARN
RURAL ROUTE 1   MEDORA VIC.   JACKSON COUNTY   INDIANA

SURVEY NO.
IN-183

HISTORIC AMERICAN
BUILDINGS SURVEY
SHEET 1 OF 6 SHEETS

LIBRARY OF CONGRESS
INDEX NUMBER

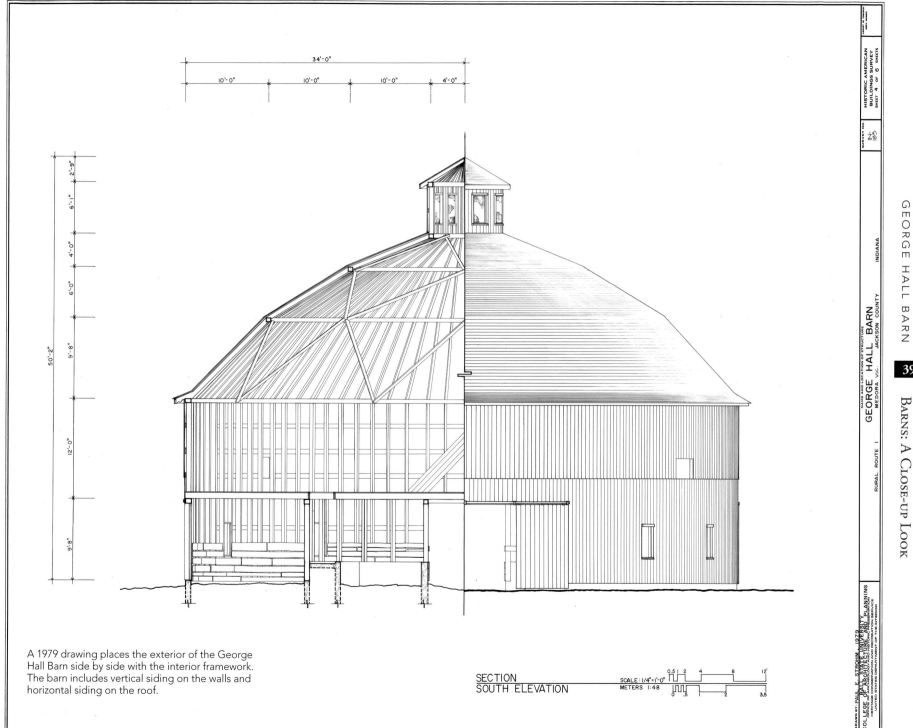

DRAWN BY: PAUL E. STROHM 1979
BALL STATE UNIVERSITY
COLLEGE OF ARCHITECTURE AND PLANNING
OFFICE OF ARCHAEOLOGY AND HISTORIC PRESERVATION
HERITAGE CONSERVATION AND RECREATION SERVICE
UNITED STATES DEPARTMENT OF THE INTERIOR

NAME AND LOCATION OF STRUCTURE
GEORGE HALL BARN
MEDORA VIC.   JACKSON COUNTY   INDIANA
RURAL ROUTE 1

SURVEY NO:
IN-
185

HISTORIC AMERICAN
BUILDINGS SURVEY
SHEET 4 OF 6 SHEETS

A 1979 drawing places the exterior of the George Hall Barn side by side with the interior framework. The barn includes vertical siding on the walls and horizontal siding on the roof.

SECTION
SOUTH ELEVATION

SCALE: 1/4"=1'-0"
METERS 1:48

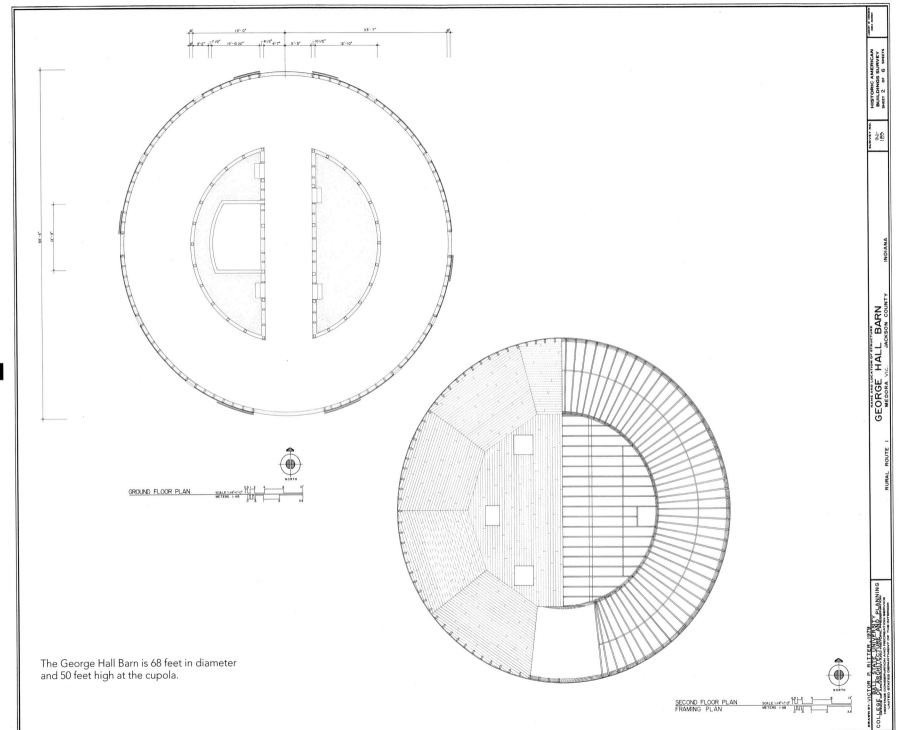

GROUND FLOOR PLAN   SCALE: 1/4"=1'-0"
METERS 1:48

NORTH

SECOND FLOOR PLAN
FRAMING PLAN   SCALE: 1/4"=1'-0"
METERS 1:48

NORTH

The George Hall Barn is 68 feet in diameter
and 50 feet high at the cupola.

DRAWN BY VICTOR P. RITTER 1979
BALL STATE UNIVERSITY
COLLEGE OF ARCHITECTURE AND PLANNING
DEPARTMENT OF ARCHAEOLOGY AND HISTORIC PRESERVATION
HISTORIC CONSERVATION AND RECREATION SERVICE
UNITED STATES DEPARTMENT OF THE INTERIOR

NAME AND LOCATION OF STRUCTURE
GEORGE HALL BARN
MEDORA VIC.   JACKSON COUNTY
RURAL ROUTE 1   INDIANA

SURVEY NO.
IN-155

HISTORIC AMERICAN
BUILDINGS SURVEY
SHEET 2 OF 6 SHEETS

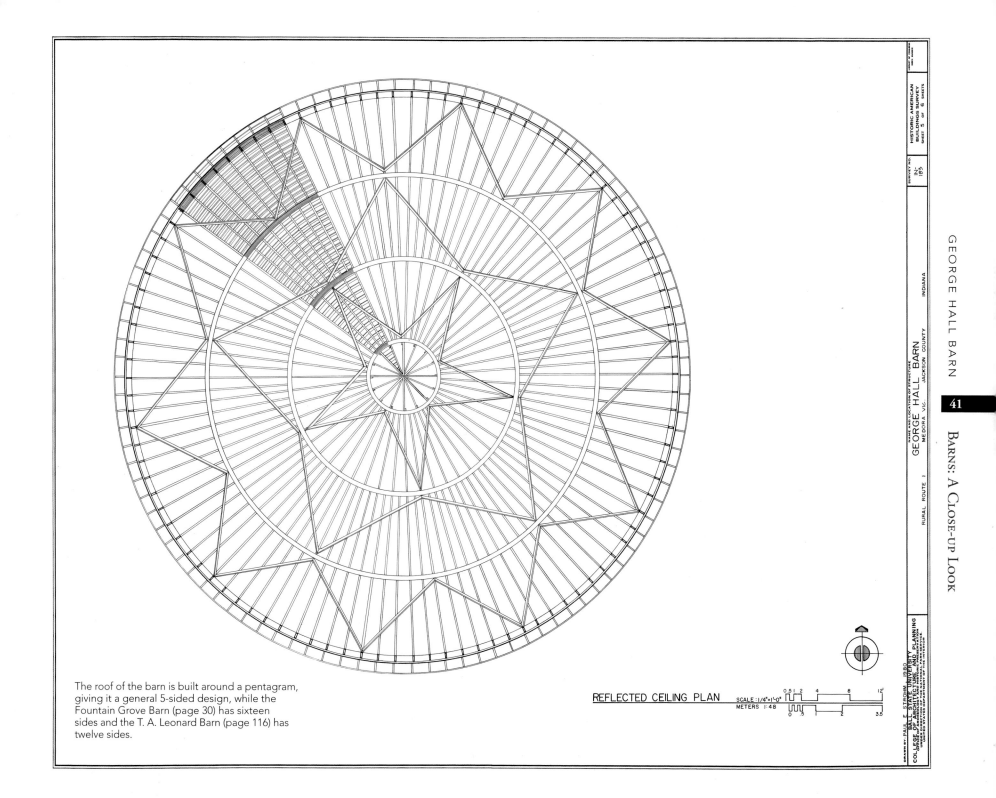

The roof of the barn is built around a pentagram, giving it a general 5-sided design, while the Fountain Grove Barn (page 30) has sixteen sides and the T. A. Leonard Barn (page 116) has twelve sides.

REFLECTED CEILING PLAN

SCALE : 1/4"=1'-0"
METERS 1:48

DRAWN BY: PAUL E. STROHM 1980
BALL STATE UNIVERSITY
COLLEGE OF ARCHITECTURE AND PLANNING
UNDER DIRECTION OF THE NATIONAL PARK SERVICE
UNITED STATES DEPARTMENT OF THE INTERIOR

NAME AND LOCATION OF STRUCTURE
GEORGE HALL BARN
MEDORA VIC.   JACKSON COUNTY   INDIANA
RURAL ROUTE 1

SURVEY NO.
IN-
185

HISTORIC AMERICAN
BUILDINGS SURVEY
SHEET 5 OF 6 SHEETS

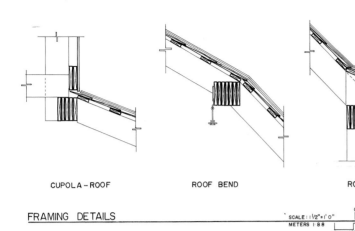

CUPOLA – ROOF   ROOF BEND   ROOF – WALL

FRAMING DETAILS

SCALE : 1 1/2" = 1' 0"
METERS 1:8.8

CENTER TRACK   MET. TRACK SUPPORT   SIDING

MISC. DETAILS

SCALE : 1 1/2" = 1'-0"
METERS 1:8.8

NOTE ALL DIAGONAL LINTEL BRACING IS 1x6

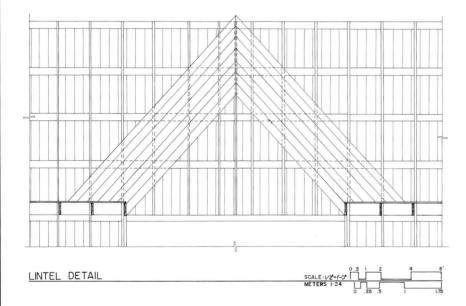

LINTEL DETAIL

SCALE : 1/2" = 1'-0"
METERS 1:24

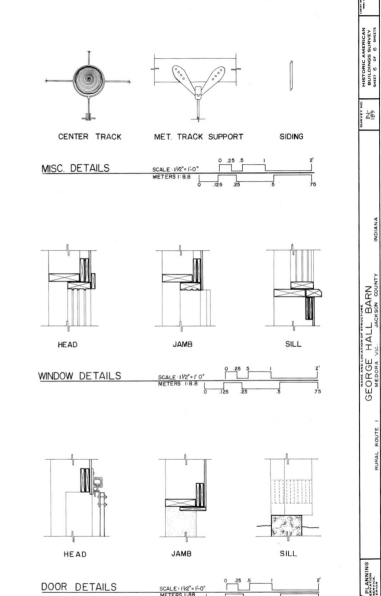

HEAD   JAMB   SILL

WINDOW DETAILS

SCALE : 1 1/2" = 1' 0"
METERS 1:8.8

HEAD   JAMB   SILL

DOOR DETAILS

SCALE : 1 1/2" = 1'-0"
METERS 1:8.8

The design of the George Hall Barn contains many intricate wooden frame joints. This drawing also includes jamb and sill details.

DRAWN BY PAUL F. STROHM 1980
BALL STATE UNIVERSITY
COLLEGE OF ARCHITECTURE AND PLANNING
OFFICE OF ARCHEOLOGY AND HISTORIC PRESERVATION
UNITED STATES DEPARTMENT OF THE INTERIOR

HISTORIC AMERICAN
BUILDINGS SURVEY
SHEET 6 OF 6 SHEETS

SURVEY NO.
IN-
185

GEORGE HALL BARN
MEDORA   VIC.   JACKSON COUNTY   INDIANA
RURAL ROUTE 1

The George Hall Barn, like many other Indiana round barns, can still be visited today.

JOHN AND MARY FELDERMAN FARM BARN

YUMA COUNTY, COLORADO · BUILT CIRCA 1908

The John and Mary Felderman Farm Barn was built circa 1908. The barn contains multiple storage rooms and a large area used for stables. A hayloft is also located along the barn's north side. Originally the farm was a horse farm, and the barn was likely used to house a portion of the horses or other livestock. Later, when the farm was converted to a dairy, a portion of the barn, once used as storage or stable space, was outfitted to be used as a milking room. The barn was constructed using wood framing and siding. The floors are all hard-packed dirt or concrete slabs. The barn also contains five Dutch animal access doors. These doors are hinged on one side and are built so the top half and bottom half can be opened separately.

SOUTH ELEVATION

SCALE: 1/4" = 1'-0"

48' - 3" (14.706m)

FEET   0 1 2 3 4   7   10

METERS 0   1   2   3   4   5

DRAWN BY: *Karen Hardaway, 1992*

ROCKY MOUNTAIN REGIONAL OFFICE/DENVER
NATIONAL PARK SERVICE
UNITED STATES DEPARTMENT OF THE INTERIOR

NAME AND LOCATION OF STRUCTURE
JOHN AND MARY FELDERMAN FARM, BARN · c.1908
VICINITY OF CLARKVILLE   YUMA COUNTY

SURVEY NO.
CO-129-B   COLORADO

HISTORIC AMERICAN BUILDINGS SURVEY
SHEET 1 OF 1 SHEETS

LIBRARY OF CONGRESS INDEX NUMBER

44

Minor alterations converted the interior of the John and Mary Felderman Farm Barn for use as a milking barn, but the exterior remains unchanged.

The north side of the barn contains a hayloft door and a very small roof extension, or hay door hood, used to cover the door.

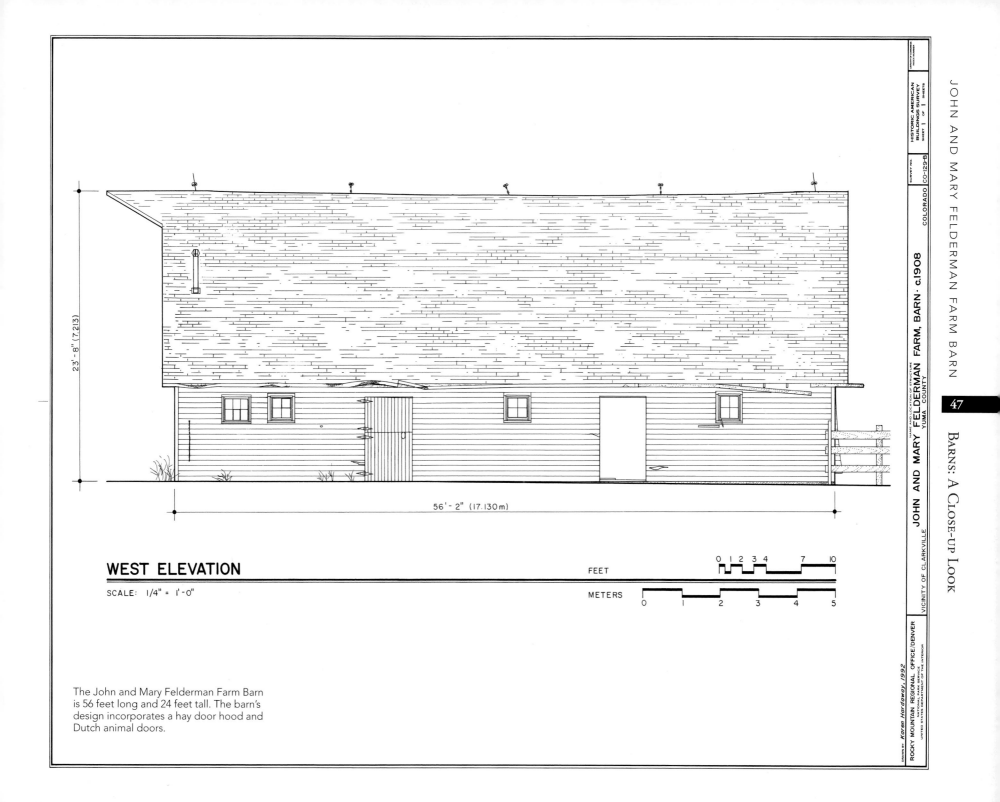

23'-8" (7.213)

56'-2" (17.130 m)

WEST ELEVATION

SCALE: 1/4" = 1'-0"

FEET

0 1 2 3 4   7   10

METERS

0   1   2   3   4   5

The John and Mary Felderman Farm Barn
is 56 feet long and 24 feet tall. The barn's
design incorporates a hay door hood and
Dutch animal doors.

HISTORIC AMERICAN
BUILDINGS SURVEY
SHEET 1 OF 1 SHEETS

SURVEY NO.
CO-129-B

COLORADO

JOHN AND MARY FELDERMAN FARM, BARN · c.1908
YUMA COUNTY

VICINITY OF CLARKVILLE

DRAWN BY: Karen Hardaway, 1992

ROCKY MOUNTAIN REGIONAL OFFICE/DENVER
NATIONAL PARK SERVICE
UNITED STATES DEPARTMENT OF THE INTERIOR

The barn stands one and a half stories high, framed with 2x6 wood beams and covered with horizontal siding.

48

The John and Mary Felderman Farm Barn includes Dutch animal doors, built with top and bottom halves that open separately, allowing light and air into the barn.

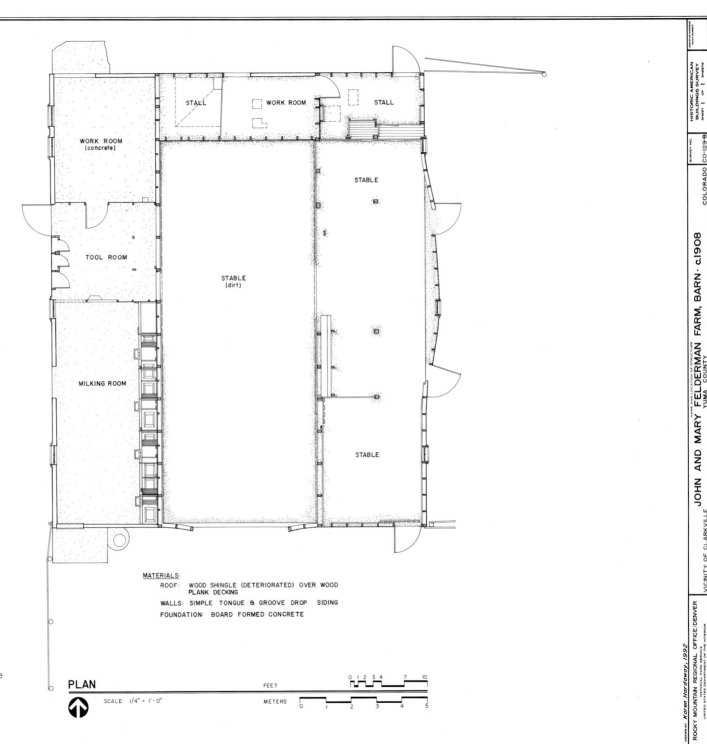

MATERIALS:

ROOF: WOOD SHINGLE (DETERIORATED) OVER WOOD PLANK DECKING

WALLS: SIMPLE TONGUE & GROOVE DROP SIDING

FOUNDATION: BOARD FORMED CONCRETE

STALL

WORK ROOM

STALL

WORK ROOM (concrete)

STABLE

TOOL ROOM

STABLE (dirt)

MILKING ROOM

STABLE

PLAN

SCALE: 1/4" = 1'-0"

FEET   0 1 2 3 4   7   10

METERS   0   1   2   3   4   5

The John and Mary Felderman Farm Barn has a board-formed concrete foundation, tongue-and-groove drop siding, and a wood-shingle roof. Inside, the barn contains stables, two workrooms, a tool room, and a milking room.

DRAWN BY: Karen Hardaway, 1992

ROCKY MOUNTAIN REGIONAL OFFICE/DENVER
NATIONAL PARK SERVICE
UNITED STATES DEPARTMENT OF THE INTERIOR

VICINITY OF CLARKVILLE   YUMA COUNTY

JOHN AND MARY FELDERMAN FARM, BARN · c.1908

NAME AND LOCATION OF STRUCTURE

HISTORIC AMERICAN BUILDINGS SURVEY
SURVEY NO. CO-129-B
COLORADO
SHEET 1 OF 1 SHEETS

The barn's hayloft includes an open space above the central aisle of the stables, making it easy to toss hay down to the ground level.

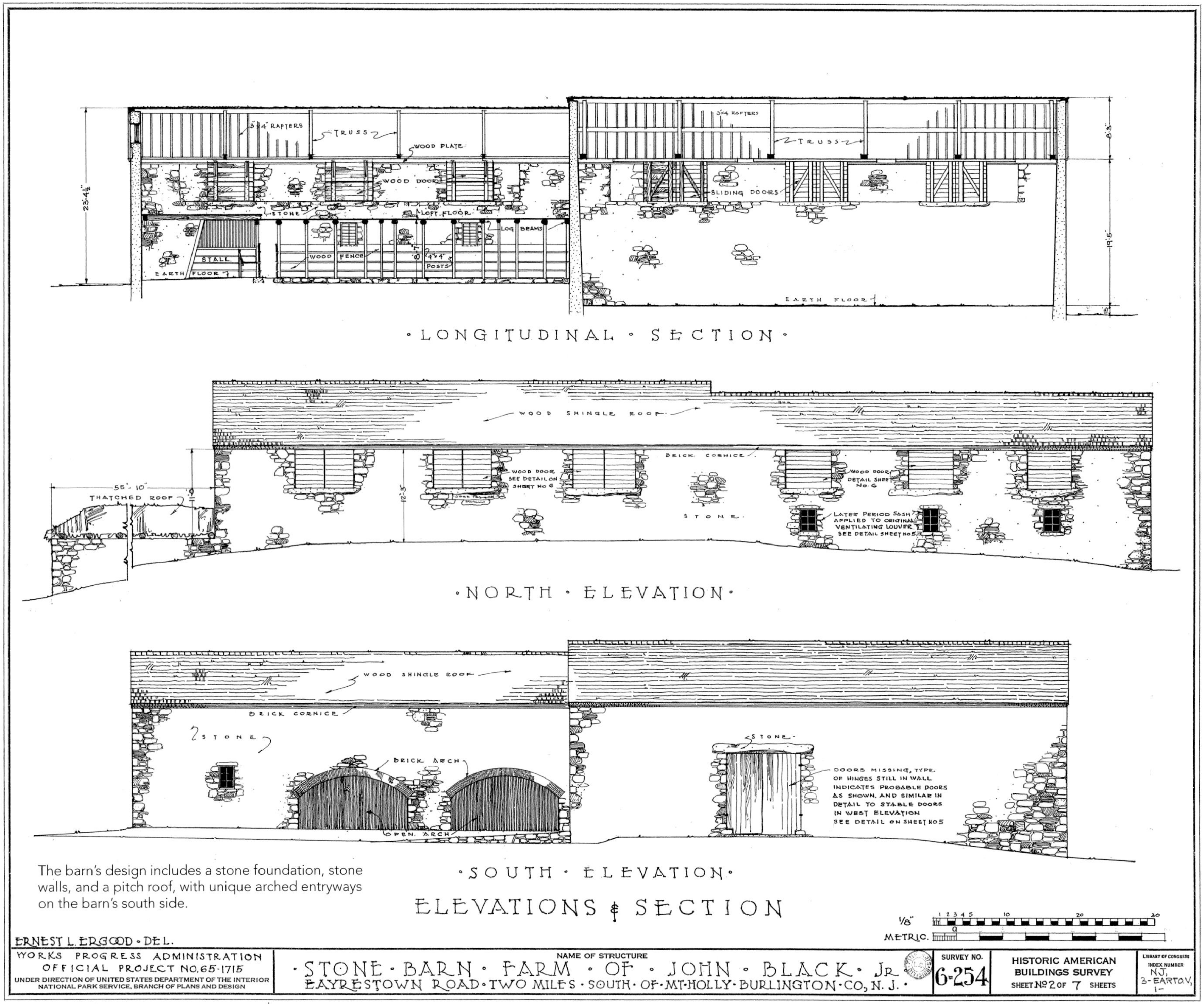

· LONGITUDINAL · SECTION ·

· NORTH · ELEVATION ·

· SOUTH · ELEVATION ·

ELEVATIONS & SECTION

The barn's design includes a stone foundation, stone walls, and a pitch roof, with unique arched entryways on the barn's south side.

ERNEST L. ERGOOD · DEL.

WORKS PROGRESS ADMINISTRATION
OFFICIAL PROJECT No. 65-1715
UNDER DIRECTION OF UNITED STATES DEPARTMENT OF THE INTERIOR
NATIONAL PARK SERVICE, BRANCH OF PLANS AND DESIGN

NAME OF STRUCTURE
· STONE · BARN · FARM · OF · JOHN · BLACK · JR ·
EAYRESTOWN ROAD · TWO MILES · SOUTH · OF · MT· HOLLY · BURLINGTON · CO·, N.J·

SURVEY No.
6-254

HISTORIC AMERICAN
BUILDINGS SURVEY
SHEET No 2 OF 7 SHEETS

LIBRARY OF CONGRESS
INDEX NUMBER
NJ,
3-EARTO.V,
1-

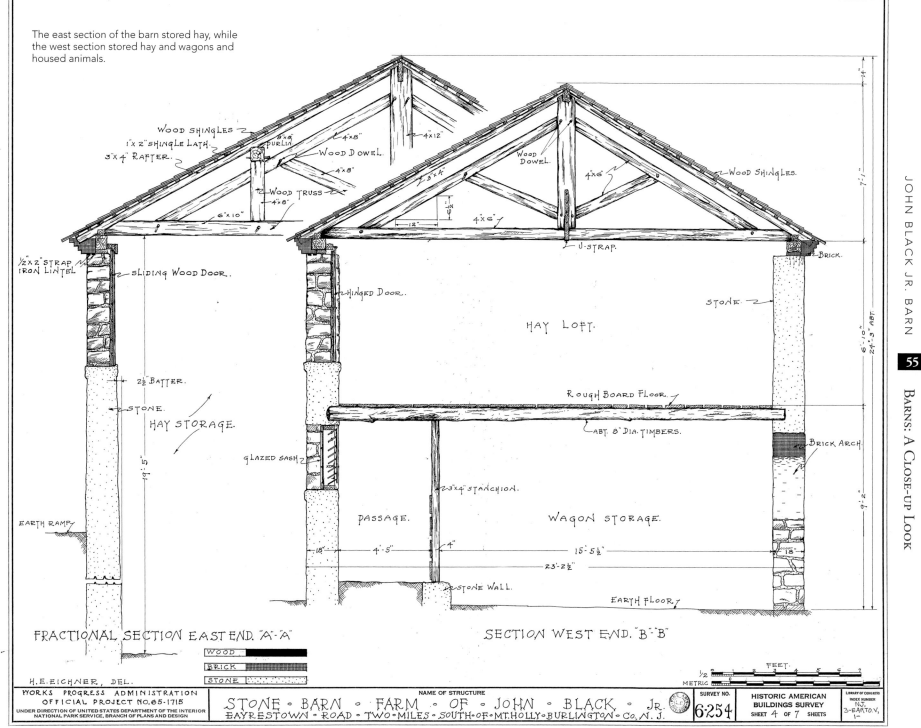

The east section of the barn stored hay, while the west section stored hay and wagons and housed animals.

WOOD SHINGLES
1"x 2" SHINGLE LATH
3"x 4" RAFTER.
9"x 9" PURLIN
4"x 8"
WOOD DOWEL.
4"x 8"
WOOD TRUSS
4"x 8"
6"x 10"
4"x 12"
3"x 4"
WOOD DOWEL.
4"x 6"
12"
4"x 6"
WOOD SHINGLES
U-STRAP.
BRICK.
½"x 2" STRAP IRON LINTEL
SLIDING WOOD DOOR.
HINGED DOOR.
HAY LOFT.
STONE
2½" BATTER.
STONE.
HAY STORAGE.
ROUGH BOARD FLOOR.
ABT. 8" DIA. TIMBERS.
GLAZED SASH
19'-5"
BRICK ARCH.
EARTH RAMP.
3"x 4" STANCHION.
PASSAGE.
WAGON STORAGE.
18"
4'-5"
4"
15'-5½"
18"
23'-2½"
STONE WALL.
EARTH FLOOR.

FRACTIONAL SECTION EAST END. "A-A"

SECTION WEST END. "B-B"

H. E. EICHNER, DEL.

WORKS PROGRESS ADMINISTRATION
OFFICIAL PROJECT NO. 65-1715
UNDER DIRECTION OF UNITED STATES DEPARTMENT OF THE INTERIOR
NATIONAL PARK SERVICE, BRANCH OF PLANS AND DESIGN

WOOD
BRICK
STONE

NAME OF STRUCTURE
STONE · BARN · FARM · OF · JOHN · BLACK · Jr.
EAYRESTOWN · ROAD · TWO · MILES · SOUTH · OF · MT. HOLLY · BURLINGTON · Co. N. J.

SURVEY NO.
6:254

HISTORIC AMERICAN
BUILDINGS SURVEY
SHEET 4 OF 7 SHEETS

LIBRARY OF CONGRESS
INDEX NUMBER
NJ.
3-EARTO. V,
1-

FEET
½
METRIC

7'-1"
14"
24'-3" ABT.
6'-10"
9'-2"

SECOND·FLOOR·PLAN

UPPER PART HAY STORAGE

Wood Truss.

"A"

HAY LOFT.

Loose Board Floor.

HAY CHUTE.

Wood Truss over.

Hay Chute.

EAVE LINE

"B" EAVE LINE

67'-7½"   127'-9"   60'-1½"

28'-8"   13'-4"   20'   13'-4"

"A"

⑤   ⑥   ⑦   ⑧   ⑨   ⑩

10'-11" 8'-0" 10'-10" 8'-1" 11'-2" 8'-4" 20'-11" 6'-2" 10'-5" 6'-1" 10'-2" 6'-0" 10'-8"

127'-9"

GROUND·PLAN

HAY STORAGE

EARTH FLOOR.

"A"

④

③

ARCHED OPENING   ARCHED OPENING

WAGON STORAGE

About 8" Dia. Logs Supporting Floor Above

PASSAGE.   LADDER.

"B"

PASSAGE.

Ladder.

②

HORSE STALL.

HORSE STALL.

①

127'-9"

35'-10½" 10'-1" 21'-8" 1'-6½" 14'-10" 6'-0" 14'-11" 8'-9" 2'-2" 11'-11"

28'-8"   21'-4"   18'

55'-10"   80'-2"   2'-1" 14'-6" 2'-2" 14'-3" 2'-3" 12'-4"

183'-7"

The east section of the barn is 68 feet long, 29 feet wide, and 29 feet tall, while the smaller west section is 60 feet long, 23 feet wide, and 23 feet tall.

LEGEND.

WOOD	
BRICK	
STONE	

H. E. EICHNER, DEL.

WORKS PROGRESS ADMINISTRATION
OFFICIAL PROJECT NO.65-1715
UNDER DIRECTION OF UNITED STATES DEPARTMENT OF THE INTERIOR
NATIONAL PARK SERVICE, BRANCH OF PLANS AND DESIGN

NAME OF STRUCTURE
STONE · BARN · FARM · OF · JOHN · BLACK · JR.
EAYRESTOWN · ROAD · TWO · MILES · SOUTH · OF · MT HOLLY · BURLINGTON · CO., N.J.

SURVEY NO.
6-254

HISTORIC AMERICAN
BUILDINGS SURVEY
SHEET 1 OF 7 SHEETS

LIBRARY OF CONGRESS
INDEX NUMBER
N.J.
3-EARTO, V,
1-

FEET.

0 2 4 6 8 10 12 14 16 18 20 22 24 26 28 30

⅛"
METRIC

Built primarily of stone, the John
Black Jr. Barn is durable and
largely safe from fire.

6-254

The barn's south side features unusual brick arched entryways.

58

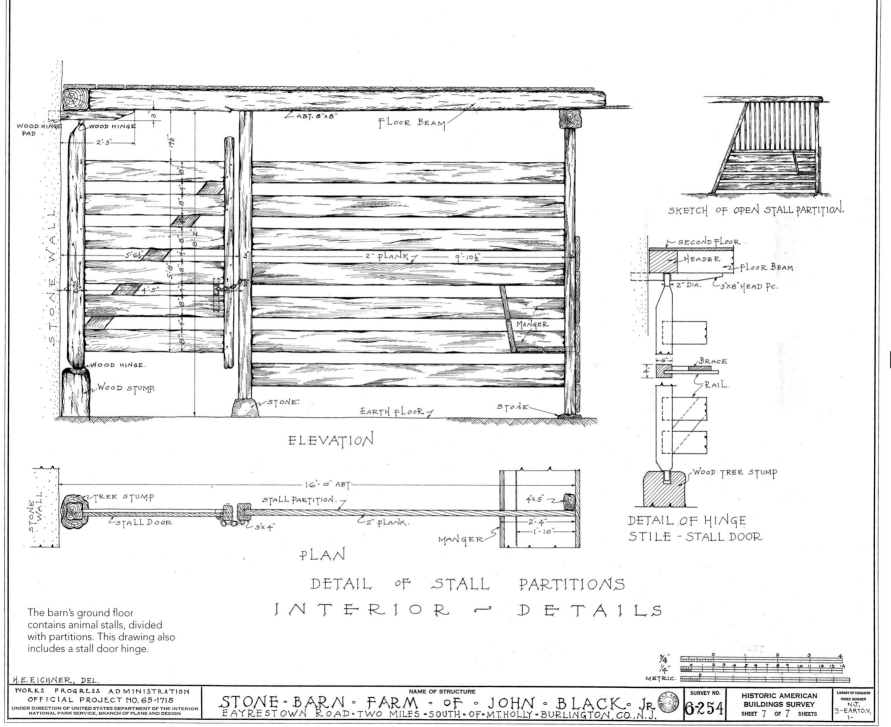

WOOD HINGE PAD

WOOD HINGE

ABT. 8"x8"

FLOOR BEAM

2'-3"

9'-2"

8"

8"-4"

8"-2"

5'-6½"

5'-8"

4'-5"

2" PLANK

9'-10½"

MANGER

STONE WALL

WOOD HINGE.

WOOD STUMP.

STONE.

EARTH FLOOR

STONE

ELEVATION

STONE WALL

TREE STUMP

STALL DOOR

3"x 4"

16'-0" ABT.

STALL PARTITION.

2" PLANK.

MANGER

4"x 5"

2'-4"

1'-10"

PLAN

DETAIL OF STALL PARTITIONS

INTERIOR ~ DETAILS

SKETCH OF OPEN STALL PARTITION.

SECOND FLOOR.

HEADER

FLOOR BEAM

2" DIA.

3"x8" HEAD PC.

6"

4"

BRACE

RAIL.

WOOD TREE STUMP

DETAIL OF HINGE
STILE - STALL DOOR

The barn's ground floor contains animal stalls, divided with partitions. This drawing also includes a stall door hinge.

¾"

¼"

METRIC.

H.E. EICHNER, DEL.

WORKS PROGRESS ADMINISTRATION
OFFICIAL PROJECT NO. 65-1715
UNDER DIRECTION OF UNITED STATES DEPARTMENT OF THE INTERIOR
NATIONAL PARK SERVICE, BRANCH OF PLANS AND DESIGN

NAME OF STRUCTURE

STONE · BARN · FARM · OF · JOHN · BLACK · JR.
EAYRESTOWN · ROAD · TWO · MILES · SOUTH · OF · MT. HOLLY · BURLINGTON · CO. · N.J.

SURVEY NO.
6-254

HISTORIC AMERICAN
BUILDINGS SURVEY
SHEET 7 OF 7 SHEETS

LIBRARY OF CONGRESS
INDEX NUMBER
N.J,
3-EARTO.V,
1-

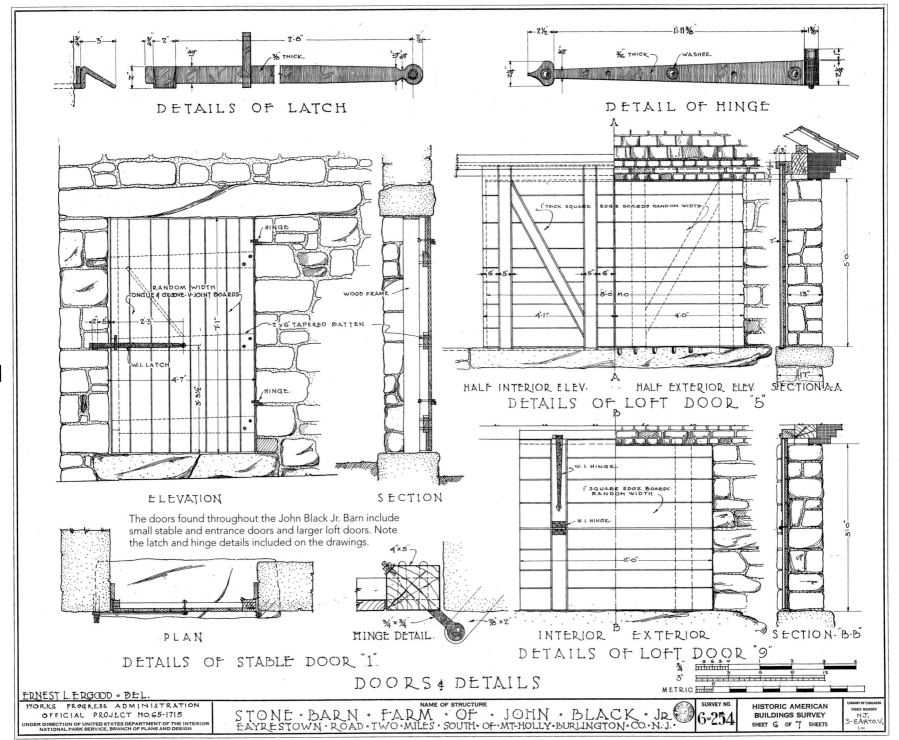

DETAILS OF LATCH

DETAIL OF HINGE

3/8 THICK

3/16 THICK   WASHER

RANDOM WIDTH
TONGUE & GROOVE-V-JOINT BOARDS

HINGE

WOOD FRAME

2 X 6 TAPERED BATTEN

W.I. LATCH

HINGE

ELEVATION

SECTION

A

1" THICK SQUARE EDGE BOARDS RANDOM WIDTH

8'-6" M.O.

4'-1"   4'-0"

5'-0"

13"

HALF INTERIOR ELEV.   HALF EXTERIOR ELEV.   SECTION A-A

A

DETAILS OF LOFT DOOR "5"

B

W. I. HINGE

1" SQUARE EDGE BOARDS
RANDOM WIDTH

W. I. HINGE

6'-0"

5'-0"

INTERIOR   EXTERIOR   SECTION B-B
B

DETAILS OF LOFT DOOR "9"

The doors found throughout the John Black Jr. Barn include
small stable and entrance doors and larger loft doors. Note
the latch and hinge details included on the drawings.

4 X 5

3/4 X 3/4   7/8 X 2"

PLAN

DETAILS OF STABLE DOOR "1"   HINGE DETAIL

DOORS & DETAILS

METRIC

ERNEST L. ERGOOD · DEL.

WORKS   PROGRESS   ADMINISTRATION
OFFICIAL PROJECT NO. 65-1715
UNDER DIRECTION OF UNITED STATES DEPARTMENT OF THE INTERIOR
NATIONAL PARK SERVICE, BRANCH OF PLANS AND DESIGN

NAME OF STRUCTURE
STONE · BARN · FARM · OF · JOHN · BLACK · JR
EAYRESTOWN · ROAD · TWO · MILES · SOUTH · OF · MT · HOLLY · BURLINGTON · CO · N.J.

SURVEY NO.
6-254

HISTORIC AMERICAN
BUILDINGS SURVEY
SHEET 6 OF 7 SHEETS

LIBRARY OF CONGRESS
INDEX NUMBER
N.J.
3-EARTO.V.
1-

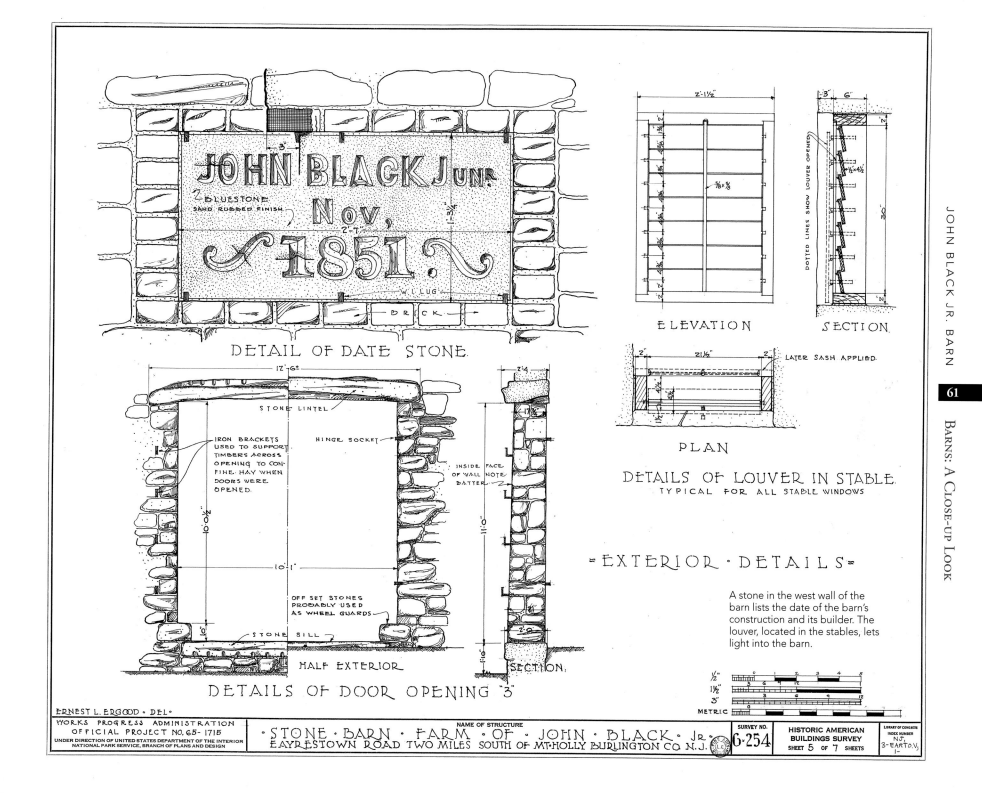

JOHN BLACK JUNR.

NOV, 27

1851.

BLUESTONE
SAND RUBBED FINISH

1-3¾

W.I. LUG

BRICK

DETAIL OF DATE STONE.

ELEVATION

5⁄8 X 5⁄8

2-1½

SECTION

DOTTED LINES SHOW LOUVER OPENED

1½ X 4½

30

PLAN

LATER SASH APPLIED.

21½

DETAILS OF LOUVER IN STABLE.

TYPICAL FOR ALL STABLE WINDOWS

17'-6"

STONE LINTEL

IRON BRACKETS
USED TO SUPPORT
TIMBERS ACROSS
OPENING TO CON-
FINE HAY WHEN
DOORS WERE
OPENED.

HINGE SOCKET

INSIDE FACE
OF WALL NOTE
BATTER

10'-0"

10'-1"

OFF SET STONES
PROBABLY USED
AS WHEEL GUARDS

STONE SILL

HALF EXTERIOR

2'-4"

SECTION

DETAILS OF DOOR OPENING "3"

EXTERIOR DETAILS

A stone in the west wall of the
barn lists the date of the barn's
construction and its builder. The
louver, located in the stables, lets
light into the barn.

½"
1½"
3"
METRIC

ERNEST L. ERGOOD · DEL·

WORKS PROGRESS ADMINISTRATION
OFFICIAL PROJECT NO. 65-1715
UNDER DIRECTION OF UNITED STATES DEPARTMENT OF THE INTERIOR
NATIONAL PARK SERVICE, BRANCH OF PLANS AND DESIGN

NAME OF STRUCTURE
·STONE· BARN· FARM· OF· JOHN· BLACK· JR·
EAYRESTOWN ROAD TWO MILES SOUTH OF MT·HOLLY BURLINGTON CO. N.J.

SURVEY NO.
6·254

HISTORIC AMERICAN
BUILDINGS SURVEY
SHEET 5 OF 7 SHEETS

LIBRARY OF CONGRESS
INDEX NUMBER
N.J,
3-EARTO.V,
1-

John R. Trimm Barn

Tishomingo County, Mississippi · Built circa 1940

John Trimm bought the tract of land that contains the John R. Trimm Barn in 1939 from D. V. Beard. Before Beard owned the property, however, the land had actually belonged to Trimm's brother-in-law, and he had lived on it for several years. John Trimm designed the barn and paid two brothers, who were just starting a carpentry business, ten cents an hour to construct the building. Trimm intended to use the barn to house registered cattle. His design featured a long hallway with a large single-room stable running along one side of the hall, and two rooms for storage along the other side. Trimm had the barn built with a gambrel roof, believing the design would allow more room for storage. Trimm filled the barn with some of the first registered cattle in the county, bringing them from Kentucky to his home in Mississippi. When the number of cattle grew too large for the barn, Trimm sold the property. Later owners would modify the barn with additions on both the north side and south side of the barn.

62

380000 E

3830000 N

TISHOMINGO 3.8 MI.

MACKEYS CREEK CH
CEM

JACKSONS CAMP CH
CEM

JOHN R. TRIMM BARN

PRENTISS CO
TISHOMINGO CO

RIDDLE CREEK

OLD NATCHEZ TRACE

MACKEYS CREEK

TAKEN FROM USGS PADEN SE QUAD UTM 16.380520.3830220

LOCATION MAP

FEET 1"=2000'
METERS 1:24000

0   3000
1 K.M.

DRAWN BY PETER DARLOW

TENNESSEE–TOMBIGBEE WATERWAY 1978
OFFICE OF ARCHEOLOGY AND HISTORIC PRESERVATION
UNDER DIRECTION OF THE NATIONAL PARK SERVICE,
UNITED STATES DEPARTMENT OF THE INTERIOR

NAME AND LOCATION OF STRUCTURE
JOHN R. TRIMM BARN
OLD NATCHEZ TRACE   TISHOMINGO VICINITY   TISHOMINGO COUNTY   MISSISSIPPI

SURVEY NO.
MISS-
181

HISTORIC AMERICAN
BUILDINGS SURVEY
SHEET 1 OF 2 SHEETS

LIBRARY OF CONGRESS
INDEX NUMBER

The structure of the John R. Trimm
Barn consists of an oak sill foundation
laid on stone pilings, pine framework
and walls, and a metal roof.

63

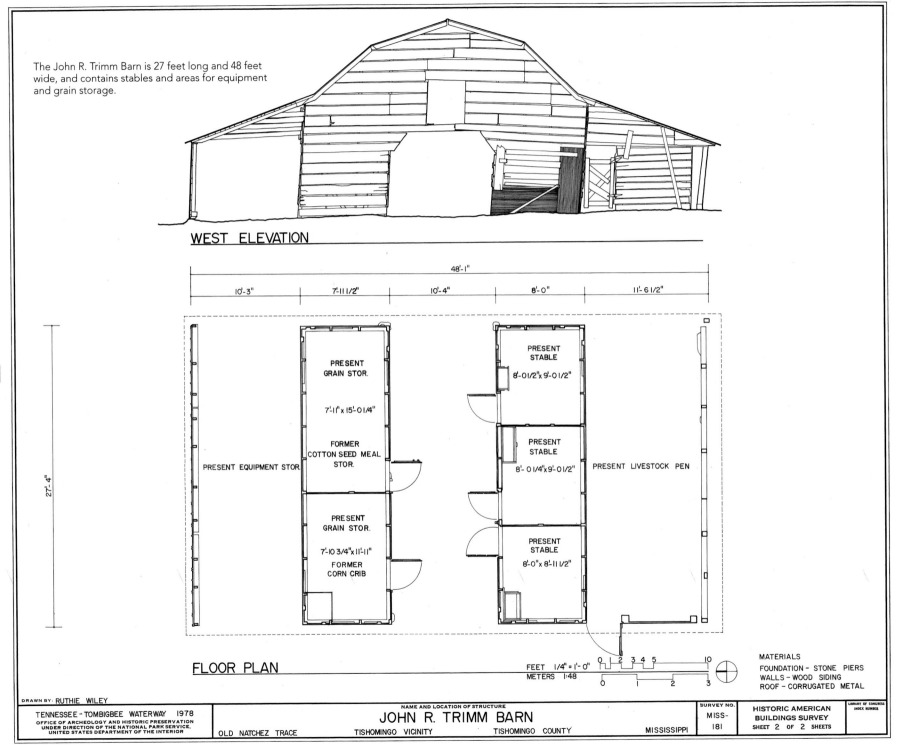

The John R. Trimm Barn is 27 feet long and 48 feet wide, and contains stables and areas for equipment and grain storage.

WEST ELEVATION

48'-1"

| 10'-3" | 7'-11 1/2" | 10'-4" | 8'-0" | 11'-6 1/2" |

27'-4"

PRESENT EQUIPMENT STOR.

PRESENT
GRAIN STOR.

7'-11" x 15'-0 1/4"

FORMER
COTTON SEED MEAL
STOR.

PRESENT
GRAIN STOR.

7'-10 3/4" x 11'-11"

FORMER
CORN CRIB

PRESENT
STABLE

8'-0 1/2" x 9'-0 1/2"

PRESENT
STABLE

8'-0 1/4" x 9'-0 1/2"

PRESENT
STABLE

8'-0" x 8'-11 1/2"

PRESENT LIVESTOCK PEN

FLOOR PLAN

FEET 1/4" = 1'-0"
METERS 1:48

0 2 3 4 5   10

0   1   2   3

MATERIALS
FOUNDATION - STONE PIERS
WALLS - WOOD SIDING
ROOF - CORRUGATED METAL

DRAWN BY: RUTHIE WILEY

TENNESSEE - TOMBIGBEE WATERWAY 1978
OFFICE OF ARCHEOLOGY AND HISTORIC PRESERVATION
UNDER DIRECTION OF THE NATIONAL PARK SERVICE,
UNITED STATES DEPARTMENT OF THE INTERIOR

NAME AND LOCATION OF STRUCTURE
JOHN R. TRIMM BARN
OLD NATCHEZ TRACE   TISHOMINGO VICINITY   TISHOMINGO COUNTY   MISSISSIPPI

SURVEY NO.
MISS-
181

HISTORIC AMERICAN
BUILDINGS SURVEY
SHEET 2 OF 2 SHEETS

LIBRARY OF CONGRESS
INDEX NUMBER

A 1978 photo includes the barn's two additions, which were added sometime after 1943.

This door is located along the barn's central aisle.

This barn's southern addition probably served as an animal pen.

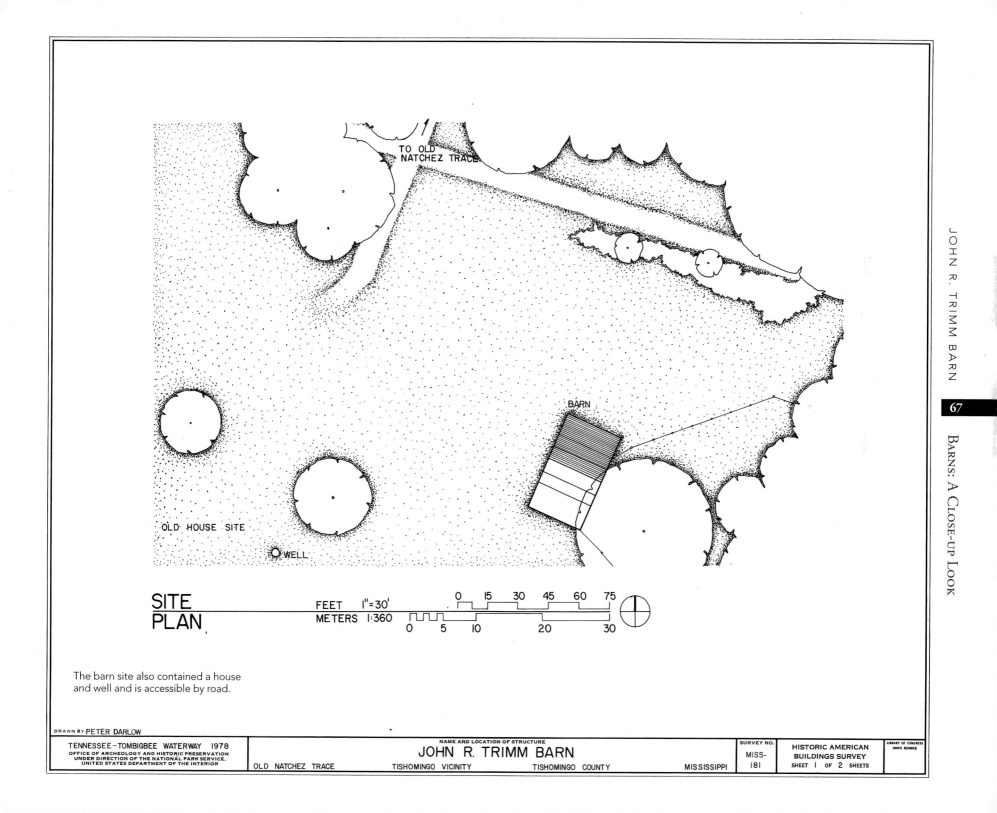

TO OLD
NATCHEZ TRACE

BARN

OLD HOUSE SITE

○ WELL

SITE
PLAN

FEET 1"=30'
METERS 1:360

0   15   30   45   60   75

0   5   10   20   30

The barn site also contained a house
and well and is accessible by road.

DRAWN BY PETER DARLOW

TENNESSEE-TOMBIGBEE WATERWAY 1978		NAME AND LOCATION OF STRUCTURE			SURVEY NO.	HISTORIC AMERICAN	LIBRARY OF CONGRESS INDEX NUMBER
OFFICE OF ARCHEOLOGY AND HISTORIC PRESERVATION UNDER DIRECTION OF THE NATIONAL PARK SERVICE, UNITED STATES DEPARTMENT OF THE INTERIOR		JOHN R. TRIMM BARN			MISS-	BUILDINGS SURVEY	
	OLD NATCHEZ TRACE	TISHOMINGO VICINITY	TISHOMINGO COUNTY	MISSISSIPPI	181	SHEET 1 OF 2 SHEETS	

Kineth Farm Barn

Island County, Washington • Built circa late 1800s

The Kineth Farm was a Donation Land Claim (DLC) property given to the Kineth family in 1853. Donation Land Claims were the result of an act of Congress passed in 1850, agreeing to give land to settlers moving into the Oregon Territory. The Kineth Farm is located on Whidbey Island, an island located just off the west coast of Washington state. The Kineths would eventually purchase an additional 160 acres of land from their neighbors, greatly expanding the farm. It is thought that the Kineth Farm was one of the first on the island to have electricity. The Kineths also utilized a complex system of pumps to supply running water to the farm. The design of the Kineth Farm Barn is similar to that of many barns in the area. It is rectangular and stands one and a half stories high. Originally, it contained animal pens and milking stalls and was used to store loose hay. Today, it has been converted into sales offices for Salmagundi Farms, but few alterations were made to the structure itself.

68

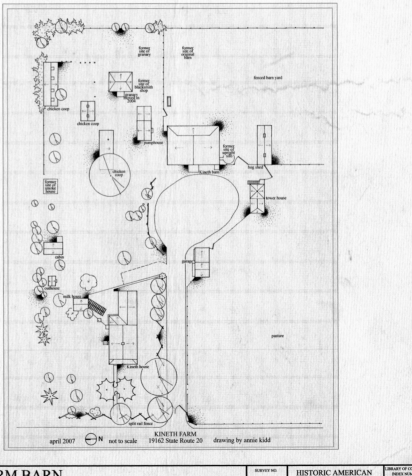

april 2007 N not to scale

KINETH FARM
19162 State Route 20

drawing by annie kidd

DRAWN BY: ANNE E. KIDD

KINETH FARM BARN, 2008
NATIONAL PARK SERVICE
U.S. DEPARTMENT OF THE INTERIOR

KINETH FARM BARN

19162 STATE ROUTE 20   COUPEVILLE   ISLAND COUNTY   WASHINGTON

SURVEY NO.
WA-248-A

HISTORIC AMERICAN
BUILDINGS SURVEY
SHEET 1 OF 2 SHEETS

LIBRARY OF CONGRESS
INDEX NUMBER

The Kineth Farm Barn has a log sill foundation and wood framing and siding. The barn received a metal roof in 1955.

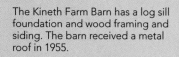

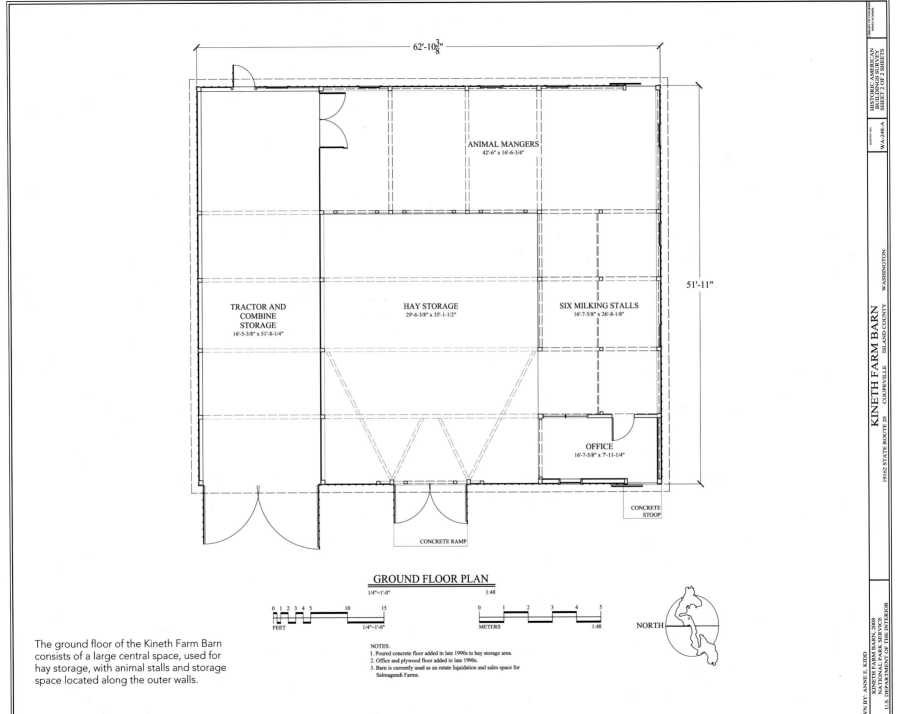

62'-10 3/8"

51'-11"

ANIMAL MANGERS
42'-6" x 16'-6-3/4"

TRACTOR AND
COMBINE
STORAGE
16'-5-3/8" x 51'-8-1/4"

HAY STORAGE
29'-6-3/8" x 35'-1-1/2"

SIX MILKING STALLS
16'-7-5/8" x 26'-8-1/8"

OFFICE
16'-7-5/8" x 7'-11-1/4"

CONCRETE
STOOP

CONCRETE RAMP

GROUND FLOOR PLAN
1/4"=1'-0"   1:48

FEET   0 1 2 3 4 5   10   15
1/4"=1'-0"

METERS   0   1   2   3   4   5
1:48

NORTH

NOTES:
1. Poured concrete floor added in late 1990s to hay storage area.
2. Office and plywood floor added in late 1990s.
3. Barn is currently used as an estate liquidation and sales space for Salmagundi Farms.

The ground floor of the Kineth Farm Barn consists of a large central space, used for hay storage, with animal stalls and storage space located along the outer walls.

HISTORIC AMERICAN BUILDINGS SURVEY
SHEET 2 OF 2 SHEETS

SURVEY NO. WA-248-A

KINETH FARM BARN

19162 STATE ROUTE 20   COUPEVILLE   ISLAND COUNTY   WASHINGTON

DRAWN BY: ANNE E. KIDD

KINETH FARM BARN, 2008
NATIONAL PARK SERVICE
U.S. DEPARTMENT OF THE INTERIOR

LIBRARY OF CONGRESS
INDEX NUMBER

71

The barn now houses sales offices for Salmagundi Farms, a company specializing in antiques and auctions.

Krämer-Witte Barn

Gasconade County, Missouri • Built between 1860 and 1865

The Krämer-Witte Barn was built by Ludwig Krämer, a shoemaker who moved from Prussia to Missouri in 1860. The barn is built along a hill, which allows access to the separate levels. The original building contained only a large threshing room with a patterned cobblestone floor with stones set in a herringbone design. A bay on its east side containing stalls and a hay mow was added later. A similar brick section was built on the barn's west side shortly after the first addition, providing more space for animal stalls and grain storage. It is known that the barn remained in use through the mid-1970s, but it is unclear whether it is still utilized today.

DRAWN BY: DONNIE G. SEALE

HERMANN MISSOURI SURVEY 1975
OFFICE OF ARCHEOLOGY AND HISTORIC PRESERVATION
UNDER DIRECTION OF THE NATIONAL PARK SERVICE,
UNITED STATES DEPARTMENT OF THE INTERIOR

NAME AND LOCATION OF STRUCTURE
KRÄMER - WITTE BARN
COUNTY RT. P   OWENSVILLE VICINITY   GASCONADE COUNTY   MISSOURI

SURVEY NO.
MO-259

HISTORIC AMERICAN
BUILDINGS SURVEY
SHEET 1 OF 8 SHEETS

LIBRARY OF CONGRESS
INDEX NUMBER

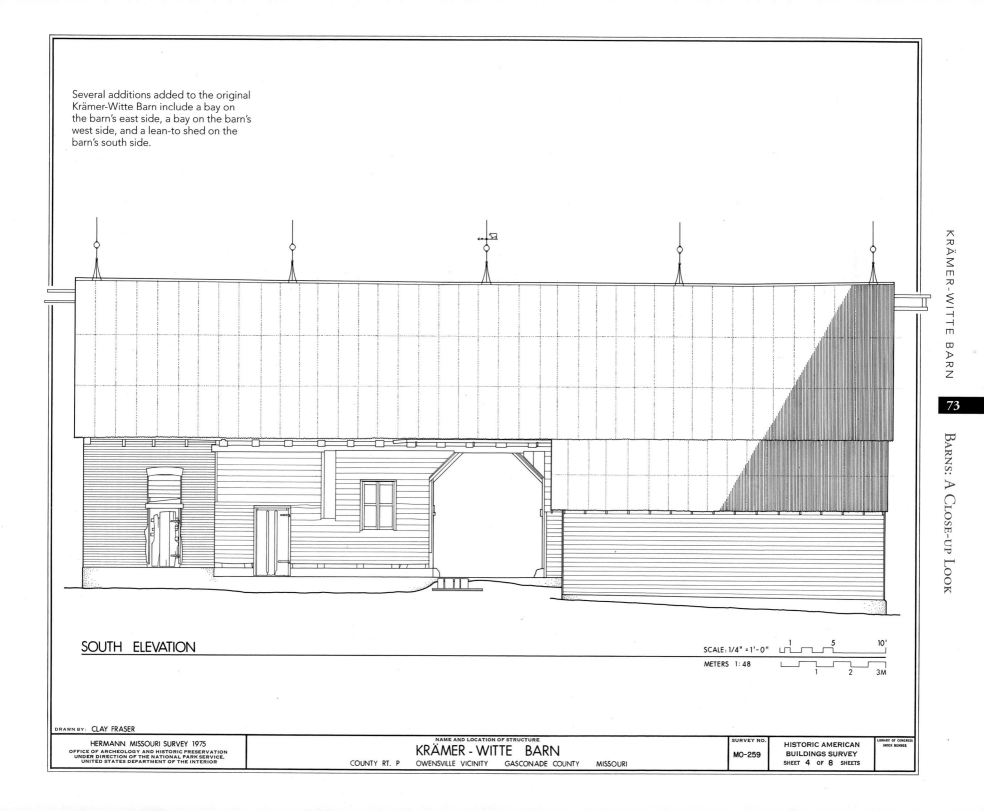

Several additions added to the original
Krämer-Witte Barn include a bay on
the barn's east side, a bay on the barn's
west side, and a lean-to shed on the
barn's south side.

SOUTH ELEVATION

SCALE: 1/4" = 1'-0"   1   5   10'

METERS 1:48   1   2   3M

DRAWN BY: CLAY FRASER

HERMANN MISSOURI SURVEY 1975
OFFICE OF ARCHEOLOGY AND HISTORIC PRESERVATION
UNDER DIRECTION OF THE NATIONAL PARK SERVICE,
UNITED STATES DEPARTMENT OF THE INTERIOR

NAME AND LOCATION OF STRUCTURE
KRÄMER - WITTE BARN
COUNTY RT. P   OWENSVILLE VICINITY   GASCONADE COUNTY   MISSOURI

SURVEY NO.
MO-259

HISTORIC AMERICAN
BUILDINGS SURVEY
SHEET 4 OF 8 SHEETS

LIBRARY OF CONGRESS
INDEX NUMBER

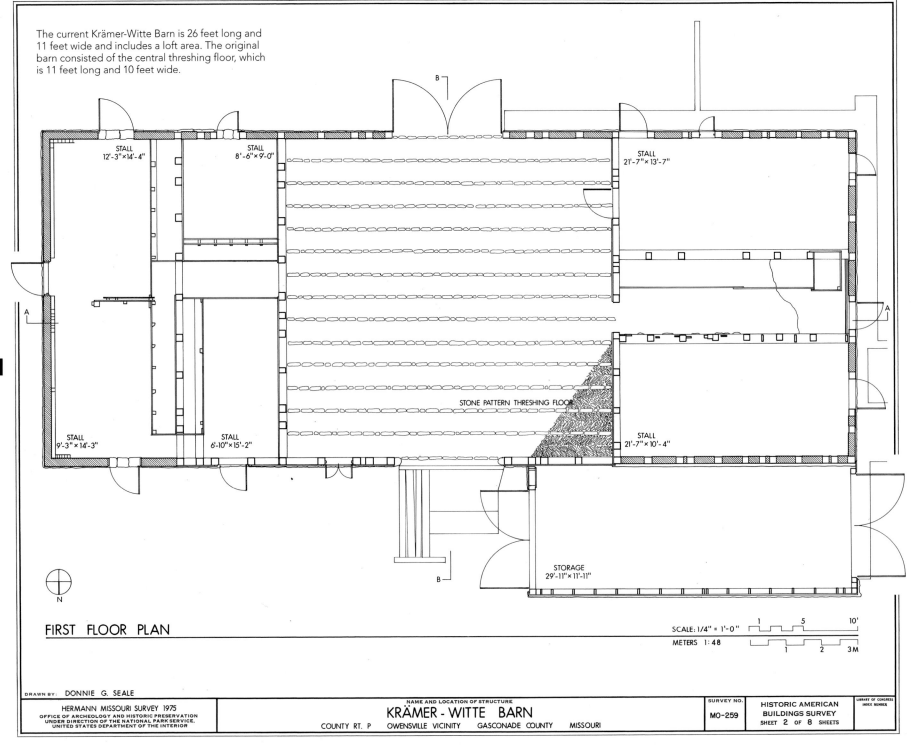

The current Krämer-Witte Barn is 26 feet long and 11 feet wide and includes a loft area. The original barn consisted of the central threshing floor, which is 11 feet long and 10 feet wide.

STALL
12'-3" × 14'-4"

STALL
8'-6" × 9'-0"

STALL
21'-7" × 13'-7"

STALL
9'-3" × 14'-3"

STALL
6'-10" × 15'-2"

STONE PATTERN THRESHING FLOOR

STALL
21'-7" × 10'-4"

STORAGE
29'-11" × 11'-11"

N

FIRST FLOOR PLAN

SCALE: 1/4" = 1'-0"

METERS 1:48

1   5   10'

1   2   3M

DRAWN BY: DONNIE G. SEALE

HERMANN MISSOURI SURVEY 1975
OFFICE OF ARCHEOLOGY AND HISTORIC PRESERVATION
UNDER DIRECTION OF THE NATIONAL PARK SERVICE,
UNITED STATES DEPARTMENT OF THE INTERIOR

NAME AND LOCATION OF STRUCTURE
KRÄMER - WITTE BARN
COUNTY RT. P   OWENSVILLE VICINITY   GASCONADE COUNTY   MISSOURI

SURVEY NO.
MO-259

HISTORIC AMERICAN
BUILDINGS SURVEY
SHEET 2 OF 8 SHEETS

LIBRARY OF CONGRESS
INDEX NUMBER

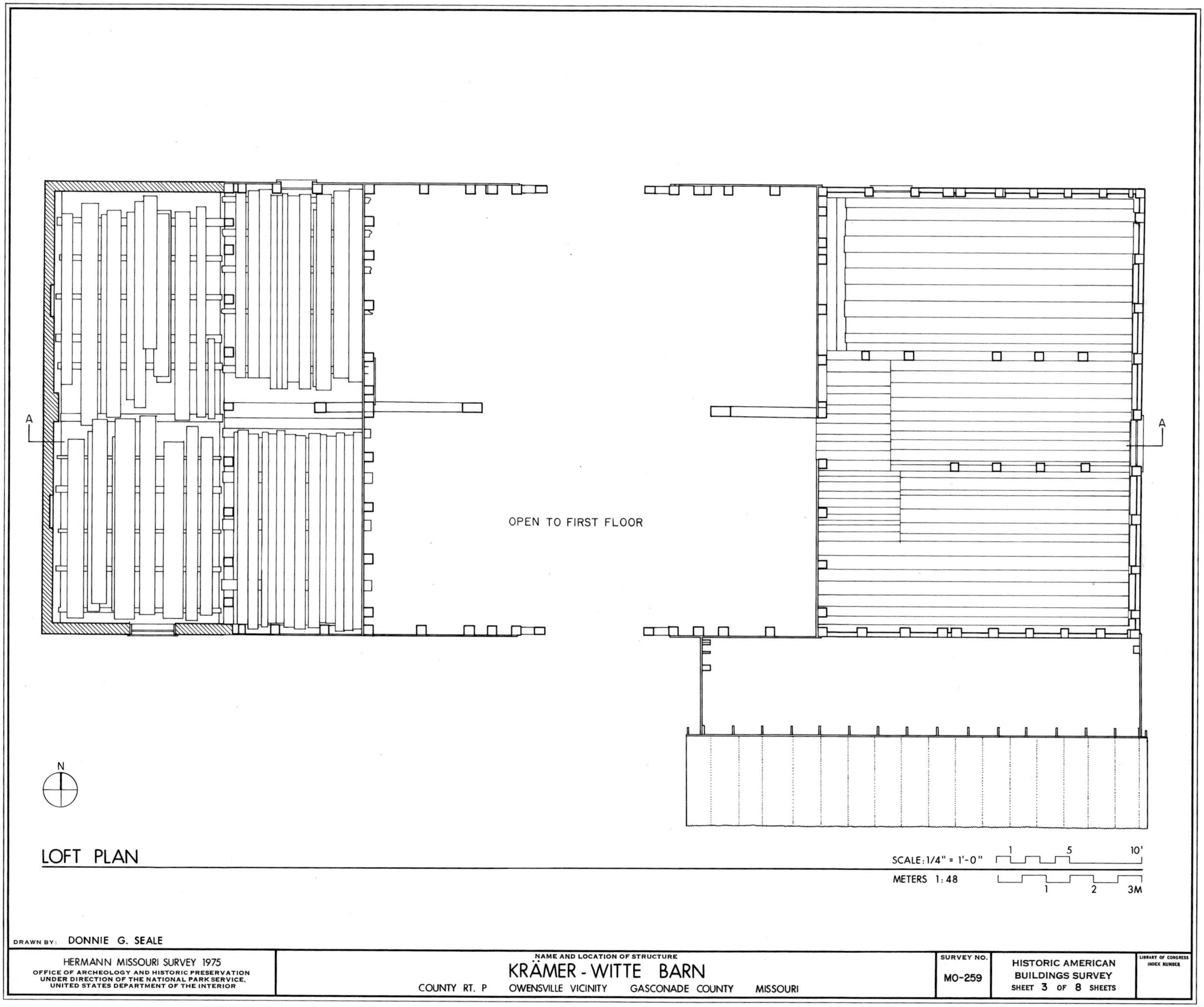

OPEN TO FIRST FLOOR

A

A

N

LOFT PLAN

SCALE: 1/4" = 1'-0"

1   5   10'

METERS 1:48

1   2   3M

DRAWN BY: DONNIE G. SEALE

HERMANN MISSOURI SURVEY 1975
OFFICE OF ARCHEOLOGY AND HISTORIC PRESERVATION
UNDER DIRECTION OF THE NATIONAL PARK SERVICE,
UNITED STATES DEPARTMENT OF THE INTERIOR

NAME AND LOCATION OF STRUCTURE
KRÄMER - WITTE BARN
COUNTY RT. P   OWENSVILLE VICINITY   GASCONADE COUNTY   MISSOURI

SURVEY NO.
MO-259

HISTORIC AMERICAN
BUILDINGS SURVEY
SHEET 3 OF 8 SHEETS

LIBRARY OF CONGRESS
INDEX NUMBER

This 1983 photo and the drawing on the facing page feature the materials used for the barn's construction. Parts of the structure consist of wood framing and siding, while other sections are brick with wood framing. The original wood-shingle roof was replaced with corrugated metal.

76

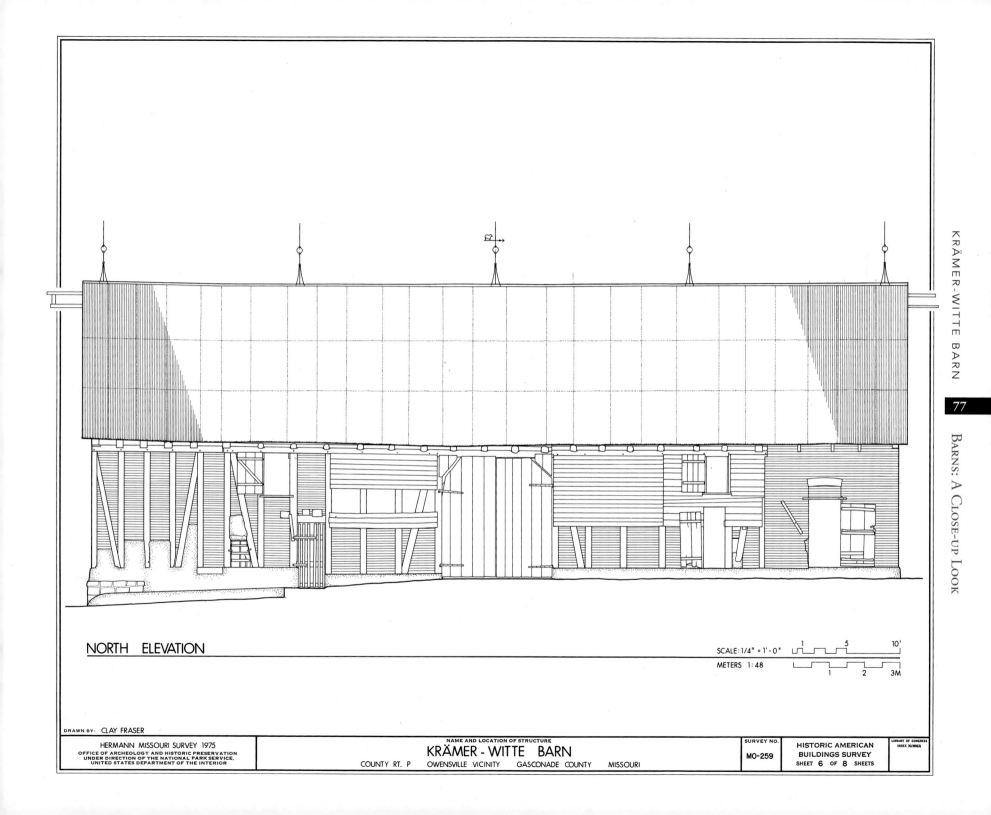

NORTH ELEVATION

SCALE: 1/4" = 1'-0"

1   5   10'

METERS 1:48

1   2   3M

DRAWN BY: CLAY FRASER

HERMANN MISSOURI SURVEY 1975
OFFICE OF ARCHEOLOGY AND HISTORIC PRESERVATION
UNDER DIRECTION OF THE NATIONAL PARK SERVICE,
UNITED STATES DEPARTMENT OF THE INTERIOR

NAME AND LOCATION OF STRUCTURE
KRÄMER - WITTE BARN
COUNTY RT. P   OWENSVILLE VICINITY   GASCONADE COUNTY   MISSOURI

SURVEY NO.
MO-259

HISTORIC AMERICAN
BUILDINGS SURVEY
SHEET **6** OF **8** SHEETS

LIBRARY OF CONGRESS
INDEX NUMBER

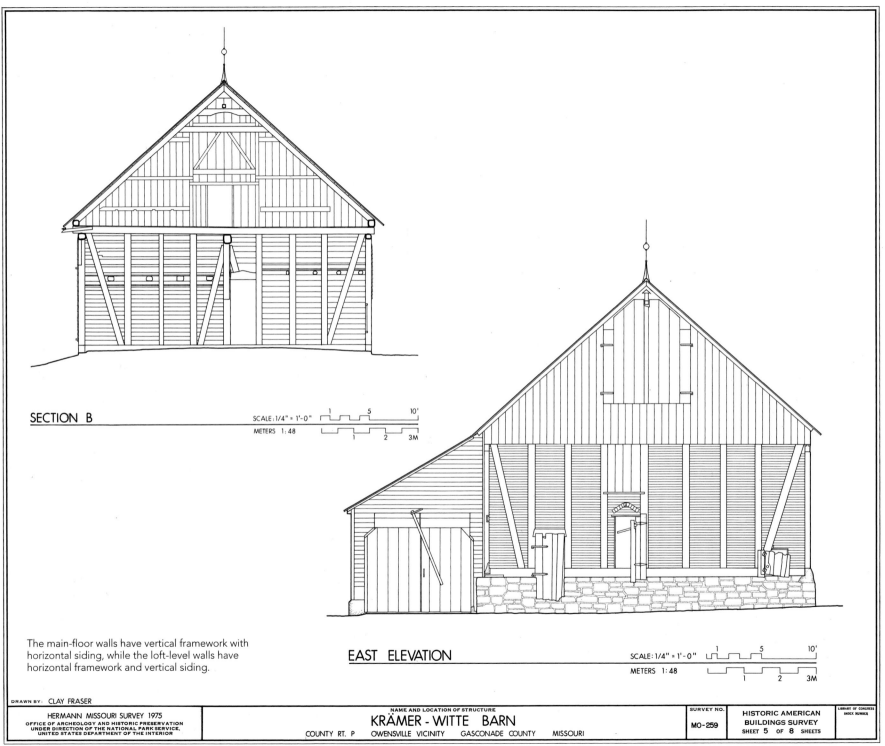

SECTION B

SCALE: 1/4" = 1'-0"

MOTORS 1:48

1   5   10'

1   2   3M

EAST ELEVATION

SCALE: 1/4" = 1'-0"

METERS 1:48

1   5   10'

1   2   3M

The main-floor walls have vertical framework with horizontal siding, while the loft-level walls have horizontal framework and vertical siding.

DRAWN BY: CLAY FRASER

HERMANN MISSOURI SURVEY 1975
OFFICE OF ARCHEOLOGY AND HISTORIC PRESERVATION
UNDER DIRECTION OF THE NATIONAL PARK SERVICE,
UNITED STATES DEPARTMENT OF THE INTERIOR

NAME AND LOCATION OF STRUCTURE
KRÄMER - WITTE BARN
COUNTY RT. P   OWENSVILLE VICINITY   GASCONADE COUNTY   MISSOURI

SURVEY NO.
MO-259

HISTORIC AMERICAN
BUILDINGS SURVEY
SHEET 5 OF 8 SHEETS

LIBRARY OF CONGRESS
INDEX NUMBER

The Krämer-Witte Barn's east side contains a large door at the loft level, providing a simple way to move materials in and out of the loft.

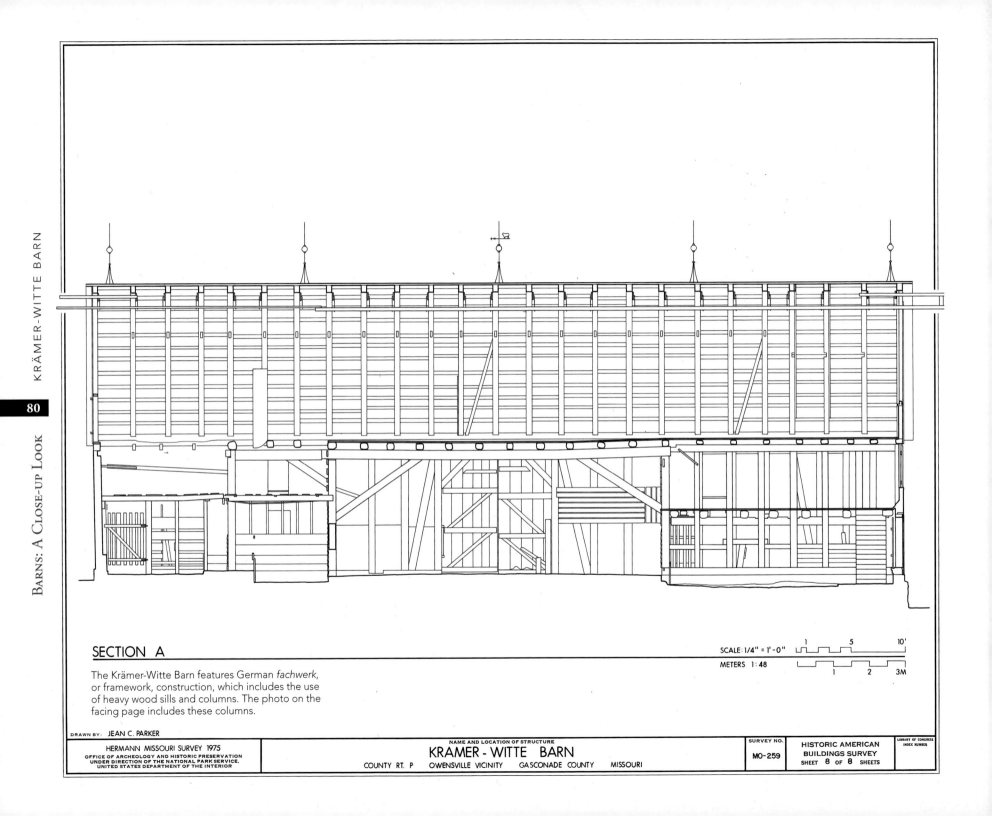

SECTION A

The Krämer-Witte Barn features German *fachwerk*,
or framework, construction, which includes the use
of heavy wood sills and columns. The photo on the
facing page includes these columns.

SCALE: 1/4" = 1'-0"

METERS 1:48

1   5   10'

1   2   3M

DRAWN BY: JEAN C. PARKER

HERMANN MISSOURI SURVEY 1975
OFFICE OF ARCHEOLOGY AND HISTORIC PRESERVATION
UNDER DIRECTION OF THE NATIONAL PARK SERVICE,
UNITED STATES DEPARTMENT OF THE INTERIOR

NAME AND LOCATION OF STRUCTURE
KRAMER - WITTE BARN
COUNTY RT. P   OWENSVILLE VICINITY   GASCONADE COUNTY   MISSOURI

SURVEY NO.
MO-259

HISTORIC AMERICAN
BUILDINGS SURVEY
SHEET 8 OF 8 SHEETS

LIBRARY OF CONGRESS
INDEX NUMBER

M. V. Riddle Barn

TISHOMINGO COUNTY, MISSISSIPPI • BUILT CIRCA 1934

M. V. Riddle constructed a log barn on his property in 1934 for use by Robert and Verlie Dean, who were renting the land. Many barns were built with logs in the 1900s so farmers could avoid milling costs. The design and construction of these barns, however, was usually poor, not like the well-constructed log cabins of the 1800s. The M. V. Riddle Barn has two levels made up of cribs and a hayloft. The cribs, located on the barn's ground level, were used to house livestock and as corncribs. Because the barn was an outbuilding and would only be used for livestock or crop storage, the spaces between the logs used to construct the barn's walls were never chinked. Instead, wooden boards were nailed to the interior of the walls to help cover the gaps. An addition, used to store equipment, was added to the barn in the late 1930s.

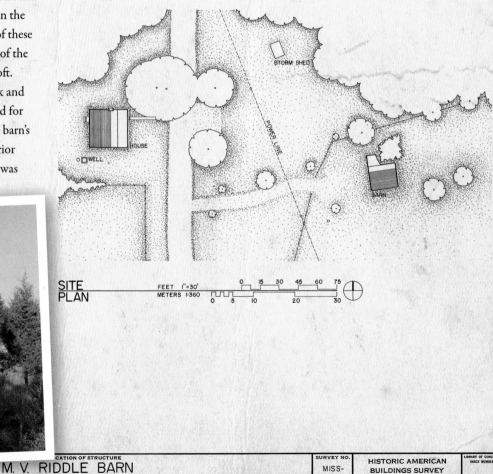

SITE PLAN

FEET 1"=30'
METERS 1:360

DRAWN BY: CAROL CRA...

TENNESSEE - TOM...
OFFICE OF ARCHEOLOG... AND HISTORIC PRESERVATION
UNDER DIRECTION OF THE NATIONAL PARK SERVICE,
UNITED STATES DEPARTMENT OF THE INTERIOR

...CATION OF STRUCTURE
M. V. RIDDLE BARN
.6 MILES WEST OF OLD NATCHEZ TRACE   TISHOMINGO VICINITY   TISHOMINGO COUNTY   MISSISSIPPI

SURVEY NO.
MISS-180

HISTORIC AMERICAN
BUILDINGS SURVEY
SHEET 1 OF 2 SHEETS

LIBRARY OF CONGRESS
INDEX NUMBER

Constructed in 1934, the
M. V. Riddle Barn acts as an
all-purpose outbuilding.

The M. V. Riddle Barn originally consisted of an enclosed building with a roofed, but open-walled, shed attached to the south side. A frame addition was added later.

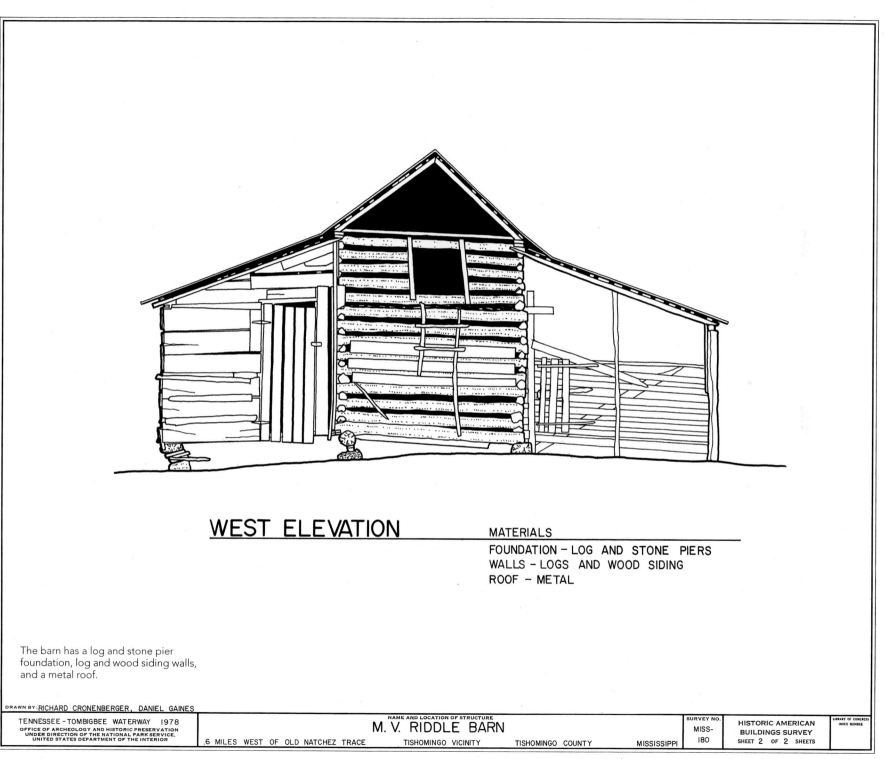

WEST ELEVATION

MATERIALS

FOUNDATION – LOG AND STONE PIERS
WALLS – LOGS AND WOOD SIDING
ROOF – METAL

The barn has a log and stone pier foundation, log and wood siding walls, and a metal roof.

DRAWN BY RICHARD CRONENBERGER, DANIEL GAINES

| TENNESSEE–TOMBIGBEE WATERWAY 1978 OFFICE OF ARCHEOLOGY AND HISTORIC PRESERVATION UNDER DIRECTION OF THE NATIONAL PARK SERVICE, UNITED STATES DEPARTMENT OF THE INTERIOR | NAME AND LOCATION OF STRUCTURE M. V. RIDDLE BARN .6 MILES WEST OF OLD NATCHEZ TRACE   TISHOMINGO VICINITY   TISHOMINGO COUNTY   MISSISSIPPI | SURVEY NO. MISS- 180 | HISTORIC AMERICAN BUILDINGS SURVEY SHEET 2 OF 2 SHEETS | LIBRARY OF CONGRESS INDEX NUMBER |

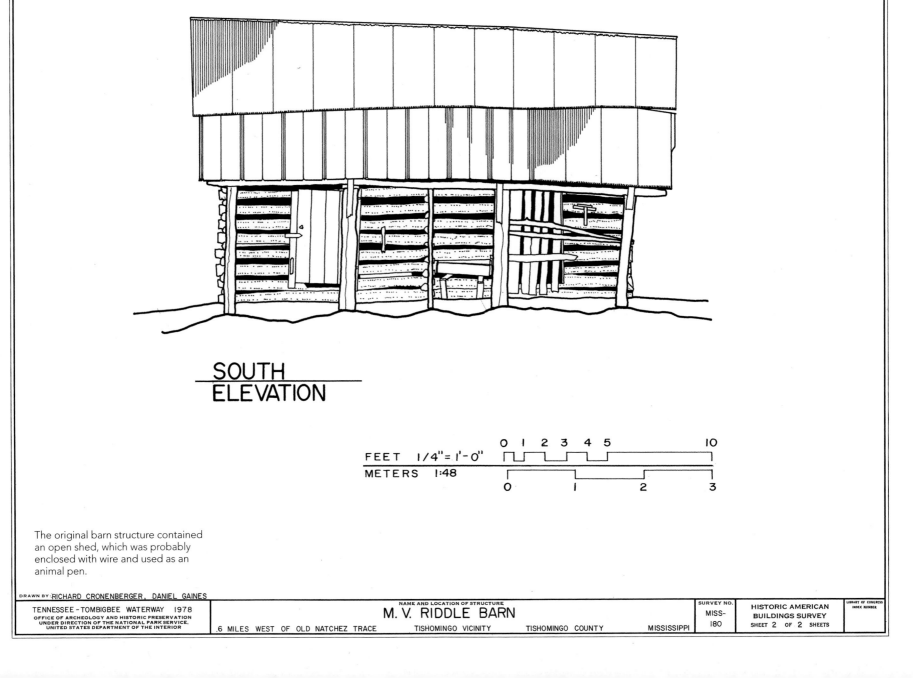

SOUTH
ELEVATION

FEET 1/4"= 1'-0"   0 1 2 3 4 5   10
METERS 1:48   0   1   2   3

The original barn structure contained
an open shed, which was probably
enclosed with wire and used as an
animal pen.

DRAWN BY: RICHARD CRONENBERGER, DANIEL GAINES

TENNESSEE - TOMBIGBEE WATERWAY 1978	NAME AND LOCATION OF STRUCTURE	SURVEY NO.	HISTORIC AMERICAN	LIBRARY OF CONGRESS INDEX NUMBER
OFFICE OF ARCHEOLOGY AND HISTORIC PRESERVATION UNDER DIRECTION OF THE NATIONAL PARK SERVICE, UNITED STATES DEPARTMENT OF THE INTERIOR	M. V. RIDDLE BARN	MISS-	BUILDINGS SURVEY	
	.6 MILES WEST OF OLD NATCHEZ TRACE TISHOMINGO VICINITY TISHOMINGO COUNTY MISSISSIPPI	180	SHEET 2 OF 2 SHEETS	

Boards nailed to the interior walls of the
M. V. Riddle Barn helped cover the
open spaces resulting from the barn's
log construction.

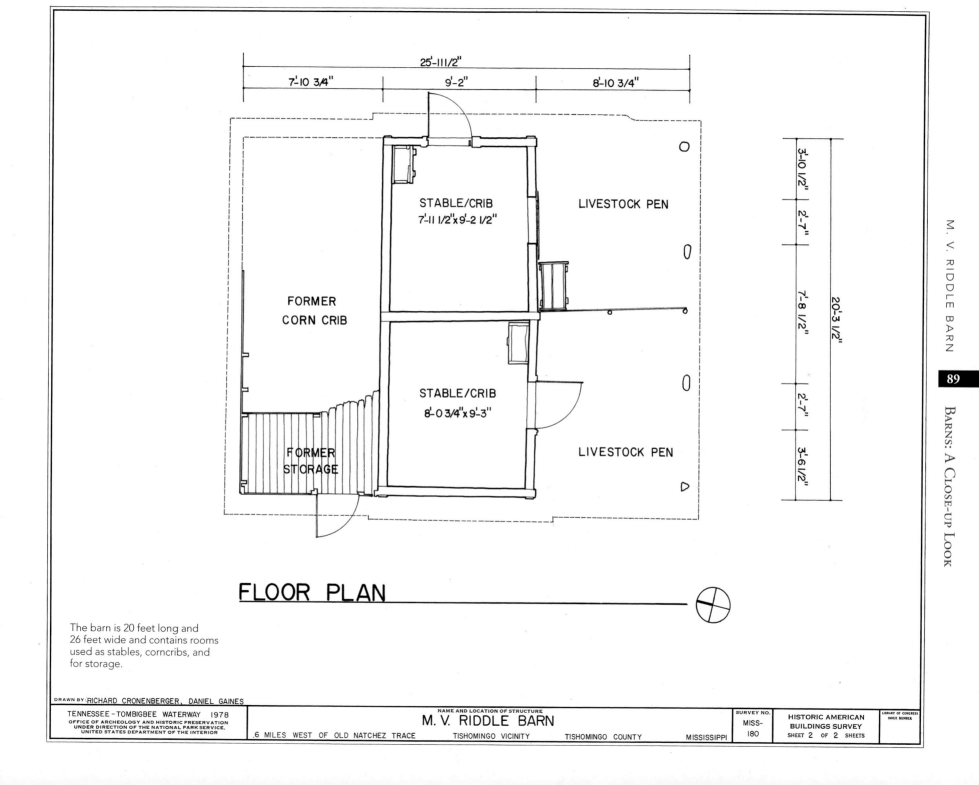

25'-11 1/2"

7'-10 3/4"   9'-2"   8'-10 3/4"

STABLE/CRIB
7'-11 1/2" x 9'-2 1/2"

LIVESTOCK PEN

FORMER
CORN CRIB

STABLE/CRIB
8'-0 3/4" x 9'-3"

FORMER
STORAGE

LIVESTOCK PEN

3'-10 1/2"
2'-7"
7'-8 1/2"   20'-3 1/2"
2'-7"
3'-6 1/2"

FLOOR PLAN

The barn is 20 feet long and
26 feet wide and contains rooms
used as stables, corncribs, and
for storage.

DRAWN BY: RICHARD CRONENBERGER, DANIEL GAINES

TENNESSEE - TOMBIGBEE WATERWAY 1978	NAME AND LOCATION OF STRUCTURE	SURVEY NO.	HISTORIC AMERICAN	LIBRARY OF CONGRESS INDEX NUMBER
OFFICE OF ARCHEOLOGY AND HISTORIC PRESERVATION UNDER DIRECTION OF THE NATIONAL PARK SERVICE. UNITED STATES DEPARTMENT OF THE INTERIOR	M. V. RIDDLE BARN .6 MILES WEST OF OLD NATCHEZ TRACE TISHOMINGO VICINITY TISHOMINGO COUNTY MISSISSIPPI	MISS-180	BUILDINGS SURVEY SHEET 2 OF 2 SHEETS	

The barn's log construction helped alleviate the cost of milling timber for the structure.

The barn's roof has square-cut timber framing, while the rest of the barn has log framing.

Reuben Ross Barn

CLAY COUNTY, MISSOURI · BUILT IN 1925

Reuben Ross and a local boy constructed the Reuben Ross Barn in 1925. Ross had purchased 140 acres of farmland in 1920 and decided to build the barn primarily for storage purposes. The barn stored equipment, food, and livestock after its completion. The barn consisted of one level, with a hayloft. It was divided into four bays, each bay being set aside for a specific purpose. The barn's gambrel roof contained a distinctive front roof extension, or hay door hood.

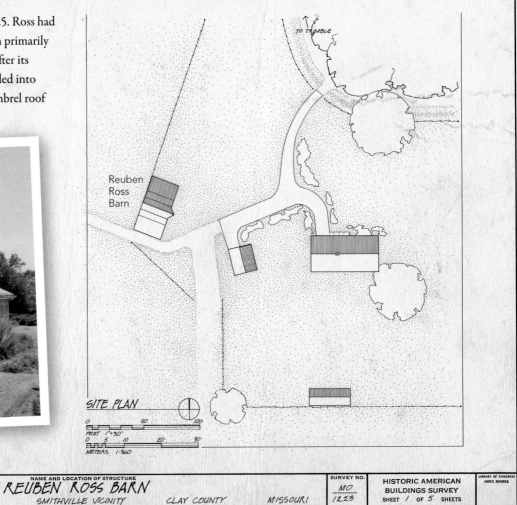

SITE PLAN

Reuben Ross Barn

TO TRIMBLE

FEET 1"=30'

METERS 1:360

DRAWN BY: DARL RASTORFER, 1978

| SMITHVILLE DAM AND RESERVOIR
OFFICE OF ARCHEOLOGY AND HISTORIC PRESERVATION
UNDER DIRECTION OF THE NATIONAL PARK SERVICE,
UNITED STATES DEPARTMENT OF THE INTERIOR | NAME AND LOCATION OF STRUCTURE
REUBEN ROSS BARN
5 MILES NORTHEAST OF SMITHVILLE   SMITHVILLE VICINITY   CLAY COUNTY   MISSOURI | SURVEY NO.
MO
1223 | HISTORIC AMERICAN
BUILDINGS SURVEY
SHEET 1 OF 5 SHEETS | LIBRARY OF CONGRESS
INDEX NUMBER |

The Reuben Ross Barn contained a front roof extension, or hay door hood, which extended over a door that opened from the hayloft. Materials were moved in and out of the barn using the door.

The barn featured wood siding nailed to wooden framing, with the exception of the north wall, which was board and batten.

94

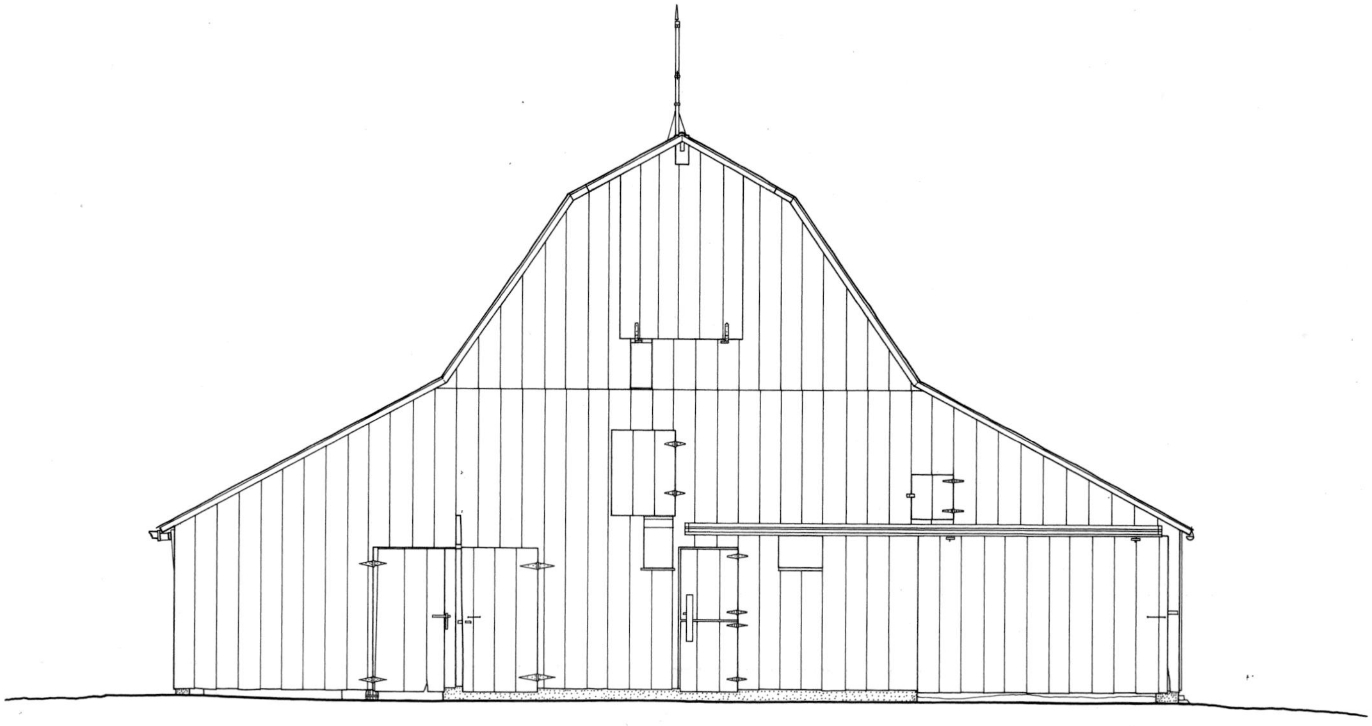

SOUTHEAST ELEVATION

This drawing includes the hayloft door
and shows the barn's vertical siding.

0 1 2 3 4 5   10
FEET: 1/4" = 1'-0"

0   1   2   3
METERS 1:48

DRAWN BY: DARL RASTORFER, 1978

SMITHVILLE DAM AND RESERVOIR
OFFICE OF ARCHEOLOGY AND HISTORIC PRESERVATION
UNDER DIRECTION OF THE NATIONAL PARK SERVICE,
UNITED STATES DEPARTMENT OF THE INTERIOR

NAME AND LOCATION OF STRUCTURE
REUBEN ROSS BARN
5 MILES NORTHEAST OF SMITHVILLE   SMITHVILLE VICINITY   CLAY COUNTY   MISSOURI

SURVEY NO.
MO
1223

HISTORIC AMERICAN
BUILDINGS SURVEY
SHEET 3 OF 5 SHEETS

LIBRARY OF CONGRESS
INDEX NUMBER

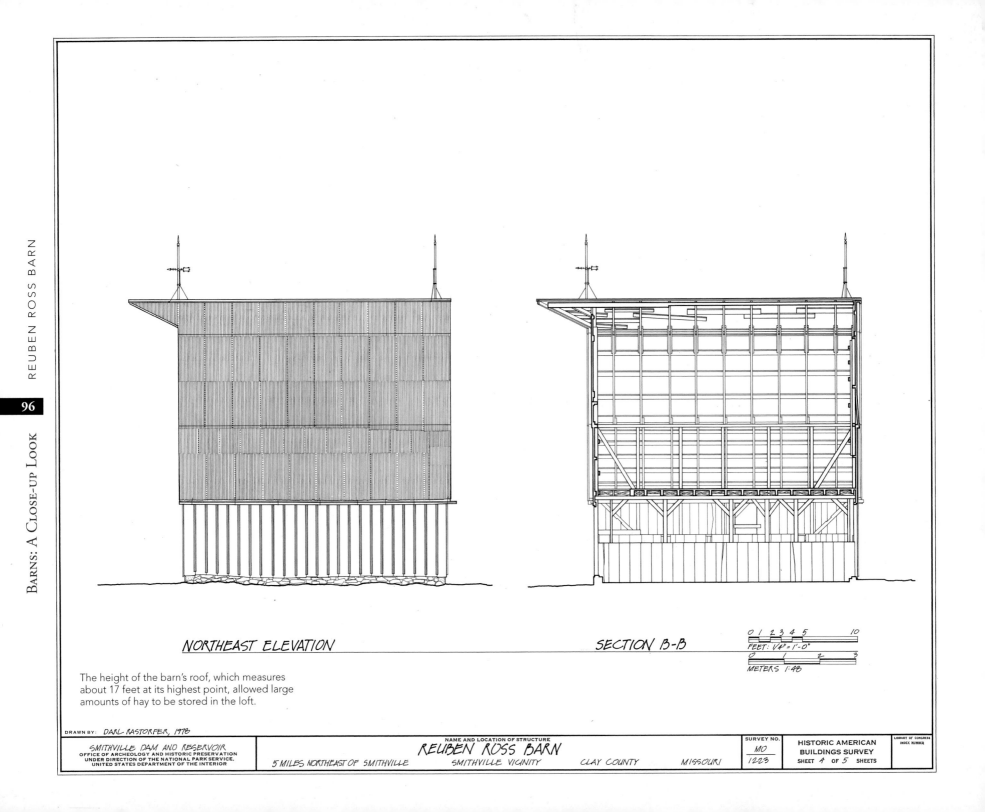

BARNS: A CLOSE-UP LOOK

NORTHEAST ELEVATION

SECTION B-B

0 1 2 3 4 5   10
FEET: 1/4" = 1'-0"

0   1   2   3
METERS 1:48

The height of the barn's roof, which measures about 17 feet at its highest point, allowed large amounts of hay to be stored in the loft.

DRAWN BY: DARL RASTORFER, 1978

SMITHVILLE DAM AND RESERVOIR
OFFICE OF ARCHEOLOGY AND HISTORIC PRESERVATION
UNDER DIRECTION OF THE NATIONAL PARK SERVICE,
UNITED STATES DEPARTMENT OF THE INTERIOR

NAME AND LOCATION OF STRUCTURE
REUBEN ROSS BARN
5 MILES NORTHEAST OF SMITHVILLE   SMITHVILLE VICINITY   CLAY COUNTY   MISSOURI

SURVEY NO.
MO
1223

HISTORIC AMERICAN
BUILDINGS SURVEY
SHEET 4 OF 5 SHEETS

LIBRARY OF CONGRESS
INDEX NUMBER

The barn was scheduled for demolition and torn down after it fell into disrepair. The land became part of the Smithville Dam and Reservoir project.

97

The barn's design utilized batten doors (left) and Dutch doors (right).

The barn has feed troughs located in several areas.

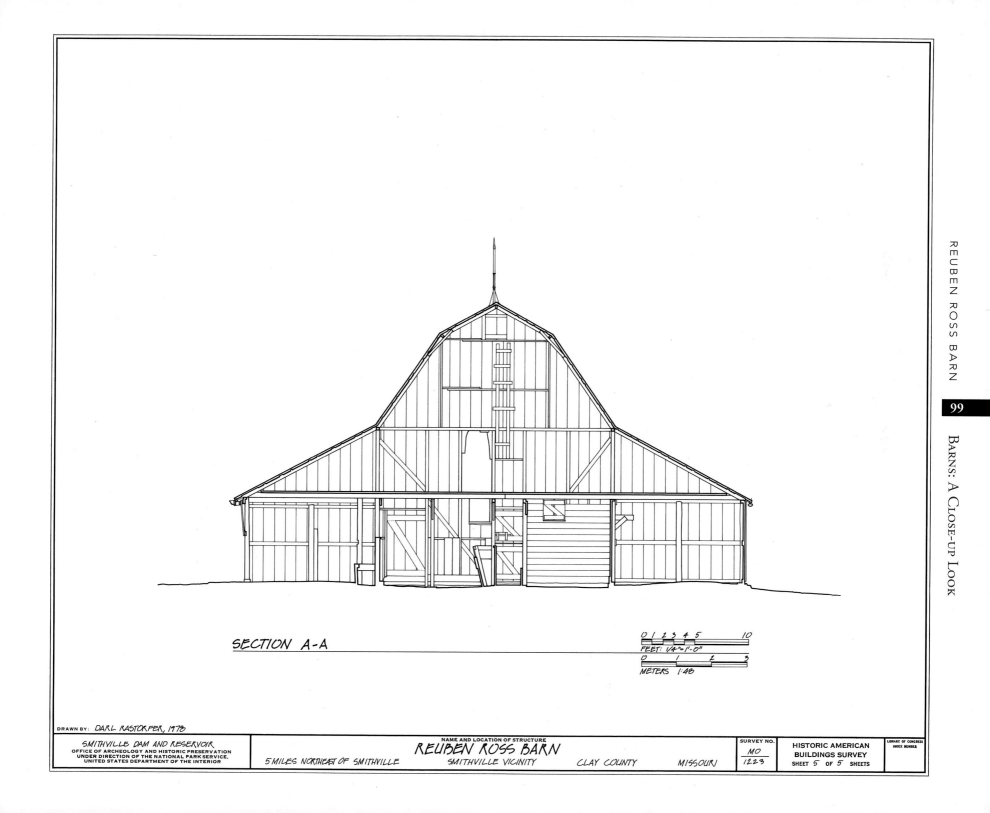

SECTION A-A

0 1 2 3 4 5   10
FEET: 1/4"=1'-0"

0   1   2   3
METERS 1:48

DRAWN BY: DARL RASTORFER, 1978

SMITHVILLE DAM AND RESERVOIR
OFFICE OF ARCHEOLOGY AND HISTORIC PRESERVATION
UNDER DIRECTION OF THE NATIONAL PARK SERVICE,
UNITED STATES DEPARTMENT OF THE INTERIOR

NAME AND LOCATION OF STRUCTURE
REUBEN ROSS BARN
5 MILES NORTHEAST OF SMITHVILLE   SMITHVILLE VICINITY   CLAY COUNTY   MISSOURI

SURVEY NO.
MO
1223

HISTORIC AMERICAN
BUILDINGS SURVEY
SHEET 5 OF 5 SHEETS

LIBRARY OF CONGRESS
INDEX NUMBER

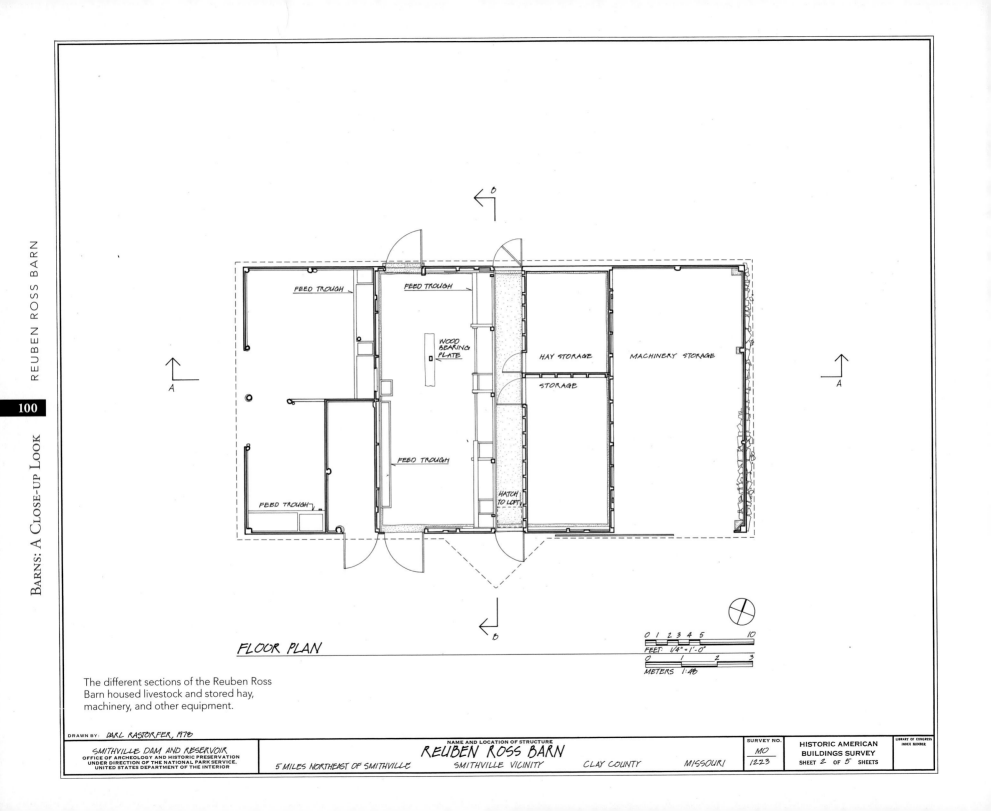

FEED TROUGH

FEED TROUGH

WOOD BEARING PLATE

HAY STORAGE

MACHINERY STORAGE

STORAGE

FEED TROUGH

FEED TROUGH

HATCH TO LOFT

FLOOR PLAN

0 1 2 3 4 5   10
FEET: 1/4" = 1'-0"

0   1   2   3
METERS 1:48

The different sections of the Reuben Ross Barn housed livestock and stored hay, machinery, and other equipment.

DRAWN BY: DARL RASTORFER, 1978

SMITHVILLE DAM AND RESERVOIR
OFFICE OF ARCHEOLOGY AND HISTORIC PRESERVATION
UNDER DIRECTION OF THE NATIONAL PARK SERVICE,
UNITED STATES DEPARTMENT OF THE INTERIOR

NAME AND LOCATION OF STRUCTURE
REUBEN ROSS BARN
5 MILES NORTHEAST OF SMITHVILLE   SMITHVILLE VICINITY   CLAY COUNTY   MISSOURI

SURVEY NO.
MO
1223

HISTORIC AMERICAN
BUILDINGS SURVEY
SHEET 2 OF 5 SHEETS

LIBRARY OF CONGRESS
INDEX NUMBER

While most gambrel roofs have sides with two slopes, a shallow upper slope and a steep lower slope, the sides of the Reuben Ross Barn roof have three slopes. The third and lowest slope extends out to the side at a low angle, providing extra storage space.

RUTHERFORD BARN

GRUNDY COUNTY, ILLINOIS • BUILT CIRCA 1830S OR 1840S

Salmon Rutherford built the Rutherford Barn directly along the I. & M. Canal in Grundy County, Illinois. The barn consists of two sections, an older section built sometime during the 1830s or 1840s, and a second section built shortly afterward. The evidence for this comes from the barn's foundation sill beams, which differ in size from the north section of the barn to the south section of the barn. This second section, which is situated directly against the canal, was likely used to house the mules that pulled boats along the canal. The barn was probably built using lumber produced at a sawmill that Rutherford also constructed and owned. Several updates were made to the barn in the early 1900s, including the addition of a drainage system and the pouring of a concrete floor. Electricity was installed some time after this.

102

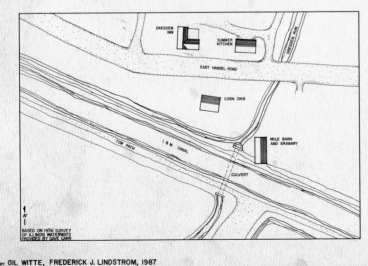

DRESDEN INN

SUMMER KITCHEN

DRESDEN RUN

EAST HANSEL ROAD

CORN CRIB

TOW PATH

I. & M. CANAL

MULE BARN AND GRANARY

CULVERT

N

BASED ON 1936 SURVEY OF ILLINOIS WATERWAYS PROVIDED BY DAVE CARR

DRAWN BY: GIL WITTE, FREDERICK J. LINDSTROM, 1987

1987 I. & M. CANAL PROJECT

NATIONAL PARK SERVICE
UNITED STATES DEPARTMENT OF THE INTERIOR

EAST HANSEL ROAD

NAME AND LOCATION OF STRUCTURE
RUTHERFORD BARN
VICINITY OF MINOOKA

GRUNDY COUNTY, ILLINOIS

SURVEY NO.
IL
1151

HISTORIC AMERICAN
BUILDINGS SURVEY
SHEET 1 OF 4 SHEETS

LIBRARY OF CONGRESS
INDEX NUMBER

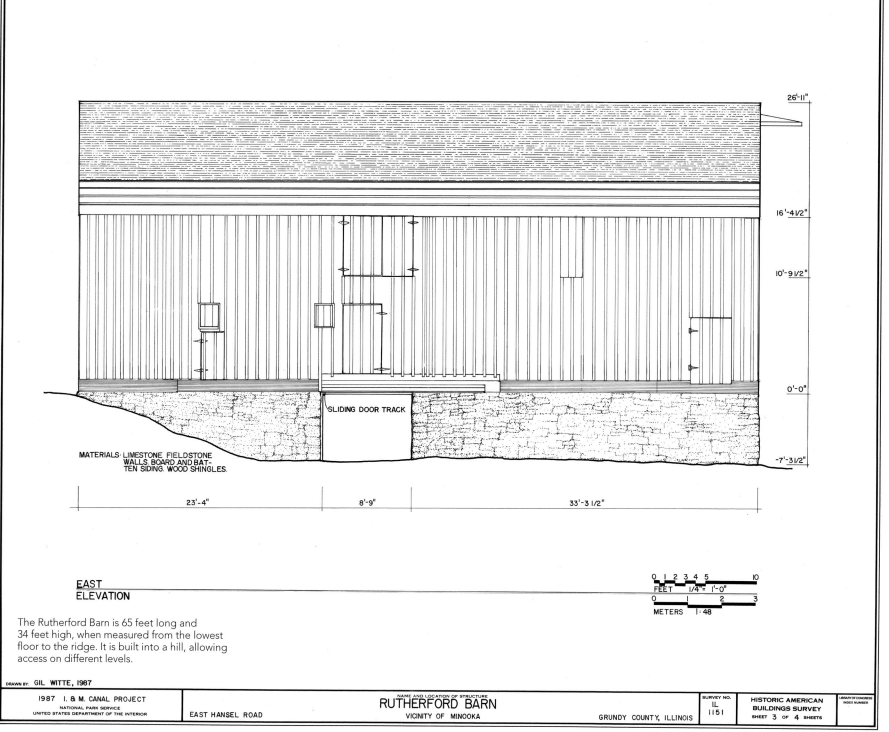

26'-11"

16'-4 1/2"

10'-9 1/2"

0'-0"

SLIDING DOOR TRACK

MATERIALS· LIMESTONE FIELDSTONE
WALLS. BOARD AND BAT-
TEN SIDING. WOOD SHINGLES.

-7'-3 1/2"

23'-4"   8'-9"   33'-3 1/2"

EAST
ELEVATION

The Rutherford Barn is 65 feet long and
34 feet high, when measured from the lowest
floor to the ridge. It is built into a hill, allowing
access on different levels.

0 1 2 3 4 5   10
FEET   1/4"= 1'-0"

0   1   2   3
METERS   1:48

DRAWN BY: GIL WITTE, 1987

1987 I. & M. CANAL PROJECT
NATIONAL PARK SERVICE
UNITED STATES DEPARTMENT OF THE INTERIOR

EAST HANSEL ROAD

NAME AND LOCATION OF STRUCTURE
RUTHERFORD BARN
VICINITY OF MINOOKA

GRUNDY COUNTY, ILLINOIS

SURVEY NO.
IL
1151

HISTORIC AMERICAN
BUILDINGS SURVEY
SHEET 3 OF 4 SHEETS

LIBRARY OF CONGRESS
INDEX NUMBER

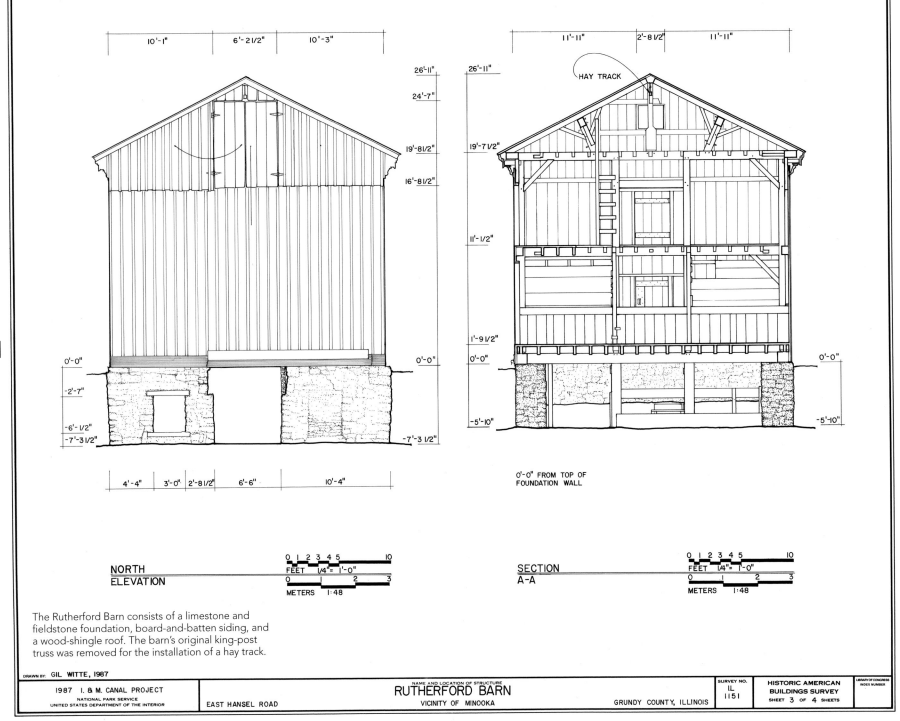

10'-1"   6'-2 1/2"   10'-3"

26'-11"
24'-7"
19'-8 1/2"
16'-8 1/2"
0'-0"
-2'-7"
-6'-1/2"
-7'-3 1/2"

0'-0"
-7'-3 1/2"

4'-4"   3'-0"   2'-8 1/2"   6'-6"   10'-4"

11'-11"   2'-8 1/2"   11'-11"

HAY TRACK

26'-11"
19'-7 1/2"
11'-1/2"
1'-9 1/2"
0'-0"
-5'-10"

0'-0"
-5'-10"

0'-0" FROM TOP OF
FOUNDATION WALL

NORTH
ELEVATION

0 1 2 3 4 5   10
FEET   1/4"= 1'-0"
0   2   3
METERS   1:48

SECTION
A-A

0 1 2 3 4 5   10
FEET   1/4"= 1'-0"
0   1   2   3
METERS   1:48

The Rutherford Barn consists of a limestone and fieldstone foundation, board-and-batten siding, and a wood-shingle roof. The barn's original king-post truss was removed for the installation of a hay track.

DRAWN BY: GIL WITTE, 1987

1987 I. & M. CANAL PROJECT
NATIONAL PARK SERVICE
UNITED STATES DEPARTMENT OF THE INTERIOR

EAST HANSEL ROAD

NAME AND LOCATION OF STRUCTURE
RUTHERFORD BARN
VICINITY OF MINOOKA

GRUNDY COUNTY, ILLINOIS

SURVEY NO.
IL
1151

HISTORIC AMERICAN
BUILDINGS SURVEY
SHEET 3 OF 4 SHEETS

LIBRARY OF CONGRESS
INDEX NUMBER

The board-and-batten siding used in the barn's construction features wide wooden siding boards with narrow wooden strips (batten) positioned over the seams between the siding.

FIELD LEVEL drawing

CONCRETE FLOOR EXTENT UNKNOWN

EVIDENCE OF MISSING SUPPORTING POSTS

15 3"x8" JOISTS

16 3"x8" JOISTS

15 3"x8" JOISTS

10"x7" COL. ON 12"x15" CONC. PIER

11"x10" COL. ON 15"x15" CONC. PIER

Dimensions (top): 10'-4"   6'-6"   2'-8 1/2"   3'-0"   4'-4"

Dimensions (right): 10'-9"   10'-9"   10'-9"   10'-0"   10'-9"   10'-9"

Dimensions (left): 34'-0"   8'-9 1/2"   23'-3"

Dimensions (bottom): 9'-3"   7'-1"   9'-1"

FEET 1/4" = 1'-0"
METERS 1:48

FIELD LEVEL

Center notes

8"x8" SILL BEAM - NORTH WALL
15"x8" SILL BEAM - EAST, WEST, & SOUTH WALL
2 12"x8" CROSS BEAMS

PERIMETER COLUMNS ARE 10 1/2" x 11". INTERIOR COLUMNS ARE 8"x 9". WALLS ARE OF LIMESTONE FIELDSTONE.

12"x8" SILL BEAMS - EAST, WEST, & SOUTH WALLS
2 12"x8" CROSS BEAMS

CANAL LEVEL drawing

OPENING TO FIELD LEVEL

4"x8" OVERHEAD LATERAL SUPPORT

10"x10 1/2" BEAMS OVERHEAD

LADDER

HAY TROUGH W/SIDE GRAIN BOXES

STALL   STALL   STALL

HAY LOFT ABOVE

GRANARY

Dimensions (top): 13'-2"   2'-8"   10'-6"

Dimensions (right): 2'-6"   3'-11"   29'-11"   3'-9"   1'-2"   1'-7 1/2"   8'-10 1/2"   1'-9 1/2"   11'-10"

Dimensions (left): 4'-3"   65'-3 1/2"   1'-7 1/2"   9'-0"   1'-7 1/2"   1'-9 1/2"

Dimensions (bottom): 3'-1"   2'-0"   6'-4"   3'-3"   3'-2"   2'-0"   6'-2"

FEET 1/4" = 1'-0"
METERS 1:48

CANAL LEVEL

The east, west, and south walls of the barn's northern section have 16-inch sill beams, while the east, west, and south walls of the south section have 13-inch sill beams.

DRAWN BY: GIL WITTE, 1987

1987 I. & M. CANAL PROJECT
NATIONAL PARK SERVICE
UNITED STATES DEPARTMENT OF THE INTERIOR

HISTORIC AMERICAN BUILDINGS SURVEY
SHEET 2 OF 4 SHEETS

SURVEY NO. IL 1151

GRUNDY COUNTY, ILLINOIS

NAME AND LOCATION OF STRUCTURE
RUTHERFORD BARN
VICINITY OF MINOOKA

EAST HANSEL ROAD

The barn received a concrete floor and electricity in the 1900s.

SHAKER CHURCH FAMILY COW BARN

GRAFTON COUNTY, NEW HAMPSHIRE · BUILT IN 1854

108

The Shaker Church Family Cow Barn, likely designed by Brother James Elkins, was built by the Enfield Brethren in 1854. The barn, like most Shaker structures, was designed to be simple, but effective. The barn, built across a gentle ravine, was carefully designed so that wagons containing supplies could enter from either end of the barn, deposit their goods, and leave by the opposite door rather than having to back in or out of a single door. Sometime after 1928, the wagon ramp on the east side of the barn was removed. During the cold months, steam was used to heat the barn's lower level, which contained stalls for cattle. Several changes were made to the barn in the 1930s. Asphalt siding was used to cover the original wooden sheathing, the cow stalls were removed, and silos were built on the surrounding land.

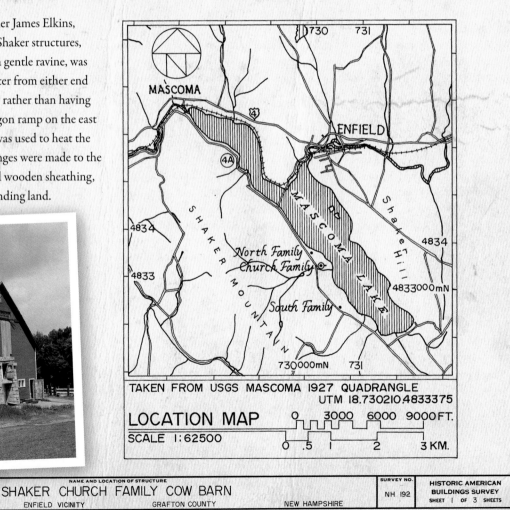

TAKEN FROM USGS MASCOMA 1927 QUADRANGLE
UTM 18.730210.4833375

LOCATION MAP
SCALE 1:62500

0   3000   6000 9000 FT.

0   .5   1   2   3 KM.

DRAWN BY:

ENFIELD PROJECT 1978
OFFICE OF ARCHEOLOGY AND HISTORIC PRESERVATION
HERITAGE CONSERVATION AND RECREATION SERVICE
UNITED STATES DEPARTMENT OF THE INTERIOR

NAME AND LOCATION OF STRUCTURE
SHAKER CHURCH FAMILY COW BARN
STATE ROUTE 4A   ENFIELD VICINITY   GRAFTON COUNTY   NEW HAMPSHIRE

SURVEY NO.
NH 192

HISTORIC AMERICAN
BUILDINGS SURVEY
SHEET 1 OF 3 SHEETS

LIBRARY OF CONGRESS
INDEX NUMBER

109

The Shaker Church Family Cow Barn includes a granite foundation, wood framing, and sections of vertical siding.

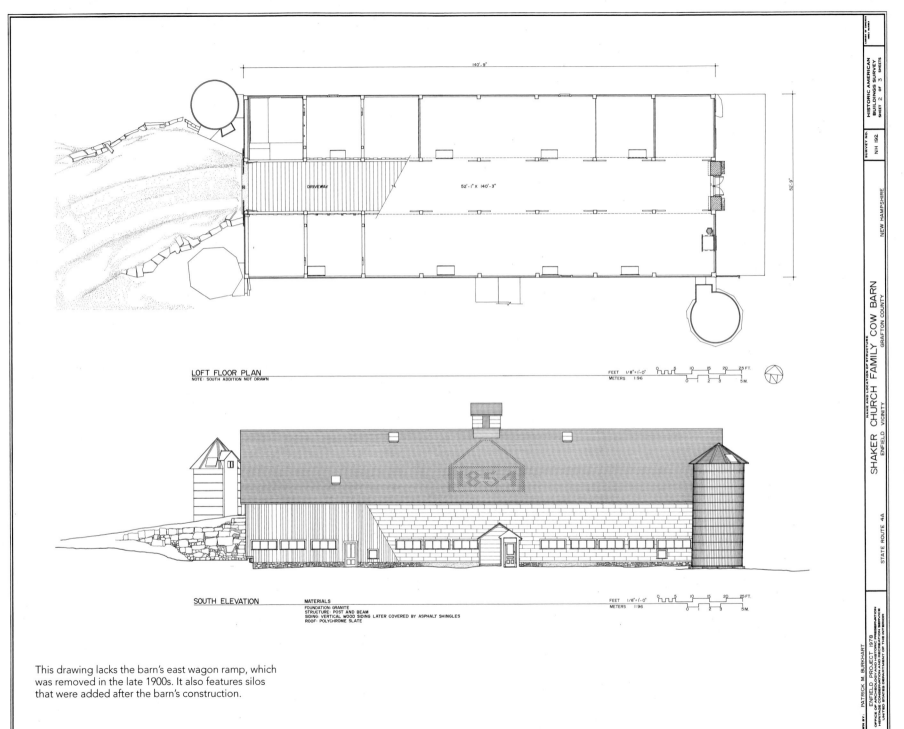

140'-9"

52'-9"

DRIVEWAY

52'-1" X 140'-3"

LOFT FLOOR PLAN
NOTE: SOUTH ADDITION NOT DRAWN

FEET 1/8"=1'-0" 0 5 10 15 20 25 FT.
METERS 1:96 0 1 2 3 5 M.

1854

SOUTH ELEVATION

MATERIALS
FOUNDATION: GRANITE
STRUCTURE: POST AND BEAM
SIDING: VERTICAL WOOD SIDING LATER COVERED BY ASPHALT SHINGLES
ROOF: POLYCHROME SLATE

FEET 1/8"=1'-0" 0 5 10 15 20 25 FT.
METERS 1:96 0 1 2 3 5 M.

This drawing lacks the barn's east wagon ramp, which
was removed in the late 1900s. It also features silos
that were added after the barn's construction.

DRAWN BY: PATRICK M. BURKHART
ENFIELD PROJECT 1978
OFFICE OF ARCHEOLOGY AND HISTORIC PRESERVATION
HERITAGE CONSERVATION AND RECREATION SERVICE
UNITED STATES DEPARTMENT OF THE INTERIOR

SHAKER CHURCH FAMILY COW BARN

STATE ROUTE 4A   ENFIELD VICINITY   GRAFTON COUNTY   NEW HAMPSHIRE

NAME AND LOCATION OF STRUCTURE

SURVEY NO.
NH 192

HISTORIC AMERICAN
BUILDINGS SURVEY
SHEET 2 OF 3 SHEETS

The polychrome slate on the barn's roof gives 1854 as the barn's construction date.

The Shaker Church Family Cow Barn was built across a small ravine, using the banks as ramps, giving wagons access to the barn from either end.

112

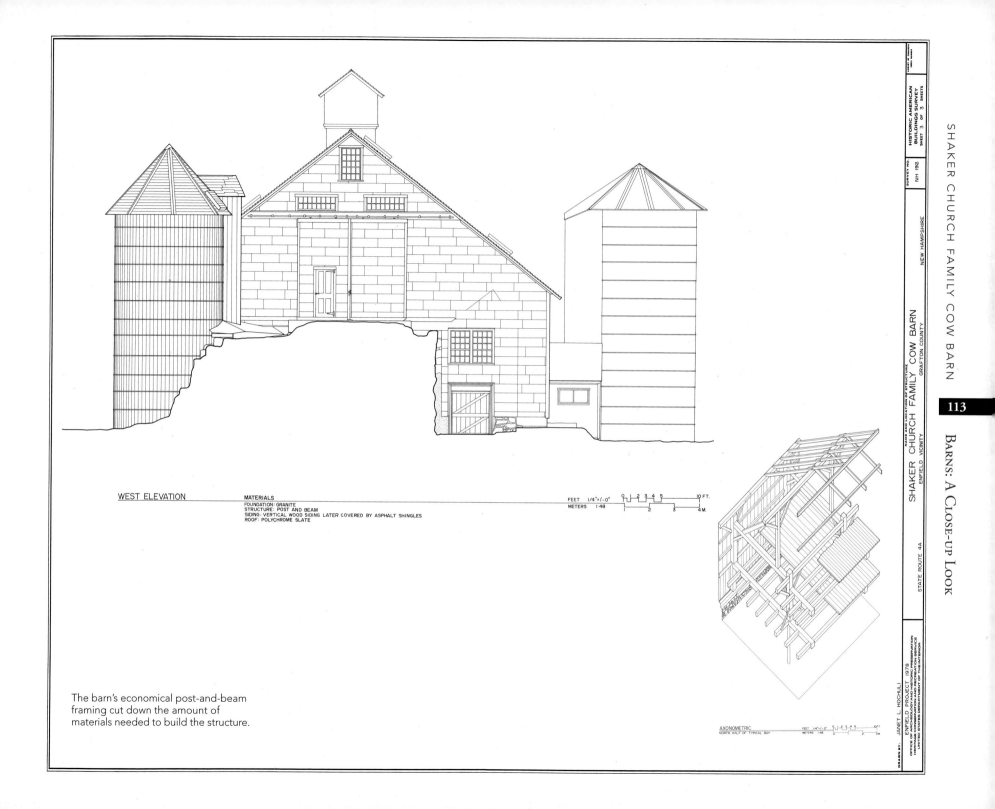

WEST ELEVATION

MATERIALS
FOUNDATION: GRANITE
STRUCTURE: POST AND BEAM
SIDING: VERTICAL WOOD SIDING LATER COVERED BY ASPHALT SHINGLES
ROOF: POLYCHROME SLATE

FEET   1/4"=1'-0"   0 1 2 3 4 5   10 FT.
METERS   1:48   1   2   3   4 M.

The barn's economical post-and-beam
framing cut down the amount of
materials needed to build the structure.

AXONOMETRIC   FEET 1/4"=1'-0" 0 1 2 3 4 5   10 FT.
NORTH HALF OF TYPICAL BAY   METERS 1:48 1   2   3   5M.

DRAWN BY: JANET L. HOCHULI

ENFIELD PROJECT 1978
OFFICE OF ARCHEOLOGY AND HISTORIC PRESERVATION
HERITAGE CONSERVATION AND RECREATION SERVICE
UNITED STATES DEPARTMENT OF THE INTERIOR

NAME AND LOCATION OF STRUCTURE
SHAKER CHURCH FAMILY COW BARN
ENFIELD VICINITY   GRAFTON COUNTY
STATE ROUTE 4A
NEW HAMPSHIRE

SURVEY NO.
NH 192
HISTORIC AMERICAN
BUILDINGS SURVEY
SHEET 3 OF 3 SHEETS

Wagons used the driveway that runs along the barn's upper level to carry supplies, farm produce, and hay into and out of the barn.

The supports for the barn's east wagon ramp remain in place, although the ramp itself was removed sometime after 1928.

A 1978 photo shows the Shaker Church Family Cow Barn after asphalt siding was added and silos were built on the site.

T. A. Leonard Barn

WHITMAN COUNTY, WASHINGTON • BUILT IN 1917

Thomas Andrew Leonard was a farmer and schoolteacher who moved from Pennsylvania to Washington. He settled near Pullman, Washington, because the area was known for its rich farmland and so he could be close to the college (today Washington State University). The barn that originally stood on his farm burned down, and he decided to replace it using the round barn design, which he had seen when travelling. It is likely that Leonard used farm periodicals to design the new round barn. The Leonard barn design differs from most other round barns, containing a greater number of windows and a higher roof height. The barn was constructed on the farm in 1917. It consists of three floors with an upper loft and was built in the shape of a dodecagon (with twelve sides).

116

VICINITY MAP

TAKEN FROM PULLMAN AND MOSCOW EAST QUADRANGLES 1975 U.T.M COORDINATES: 11-490595-5172115

PULLMAN

WASHINGTON STATE UNIVERSITY

OLD MOSCOW HIGHWAY

LEONARD BARN

GN 0° 08' 2 MILS
MN 20° 356 MILS

MILES
KILOMETERS

DRAWN BY: STEVE E. NYS, 1985

WASHINGTON STATE OFFICE OF ARCHAEOLOGY AND HISTORIC PRESERVATION
NATIONAL PARK SERVICE
UNITED STATES DEPARTMENT OF THE INTERIOR

NAME AND LOCATION OF STRUCTURE
T. A. LEONARD BARN
OLD MOSCOW HIGHWAY   PULLMAN VICINITY   WHITMAN COUNTY   WASHINGTON

SURVEY NO.
WA-168

HISTORIC AMERICAN BUILDINGS SURVEY
SHEET 1 OF 10 SHEETS

LIBRARY OF CONGRESS INDEX NUMBER

The T. A. Leonard Barn consists of a concrete foundation, timber framing, and shiplap siding.

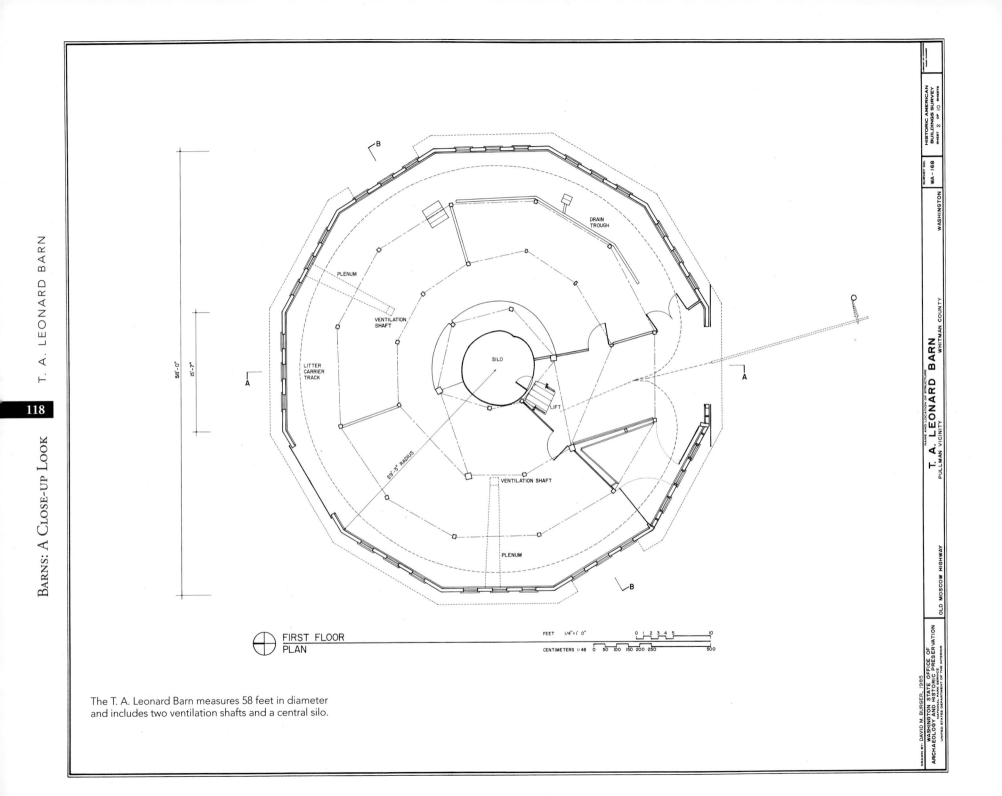

FIRST FLOOR
PLAN

The T. A. Leonard Barn measures 58 feet in diameter
and includes two ventilation shafts and a central silo.

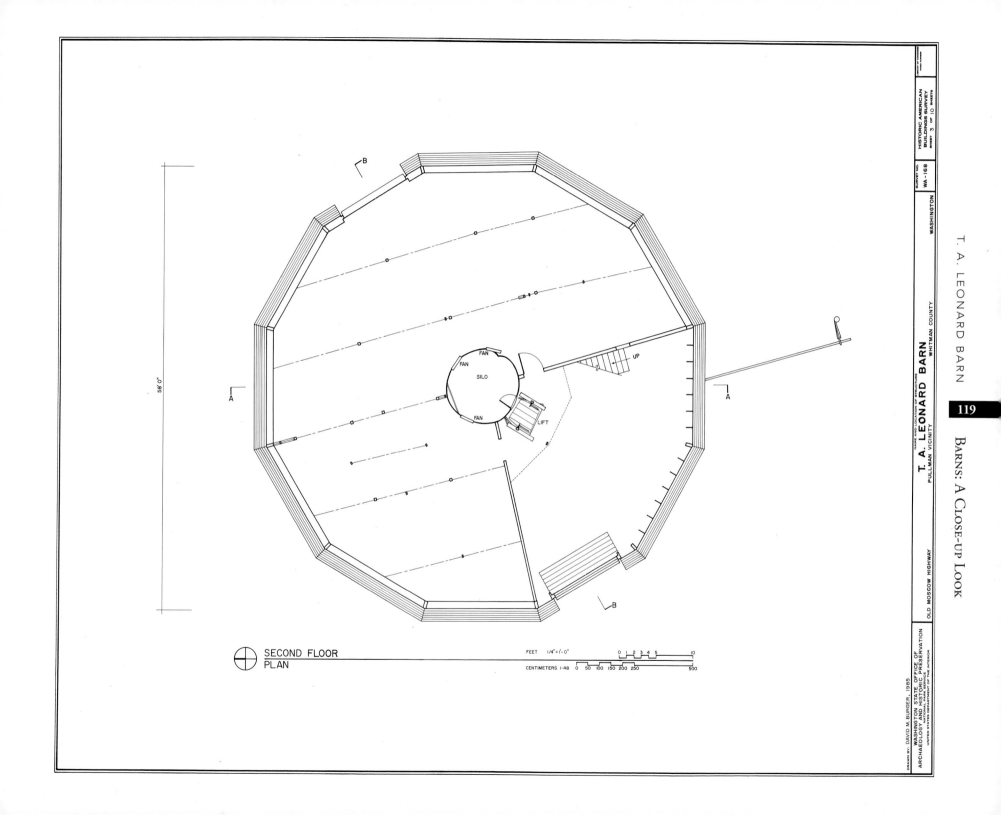

SECOND FLOOR
PLAN

58' 0"

FEET 1/4"=1'-0"

0 1 2 3 4 5   10

CENTIMETERS 1:48   0 50 100 150 200 250   500

DRAWN BY: DAVID M. BURGER, 1985

WASHINGTON STATE OFFICE OF
ARCHAEOLOGY AND HISTORIC PRESERVATION
NATIONAL PARK SERVICE
UNITED STATES DEPARTMENT OF THE INTERIOR

NAME AND LOCATION OF STRUCTURE
T. A. LEONARD BARN
PULLMAN VICINITY

OLD MOSCOW HIGHWAY   WHITMAN COUNTY

SURVEY NO.
WA-168

WASHINGTON

HISTORIC AMERICAN
BUILDINGS SURVEY
SHEET 3 OF 10 SHEETS

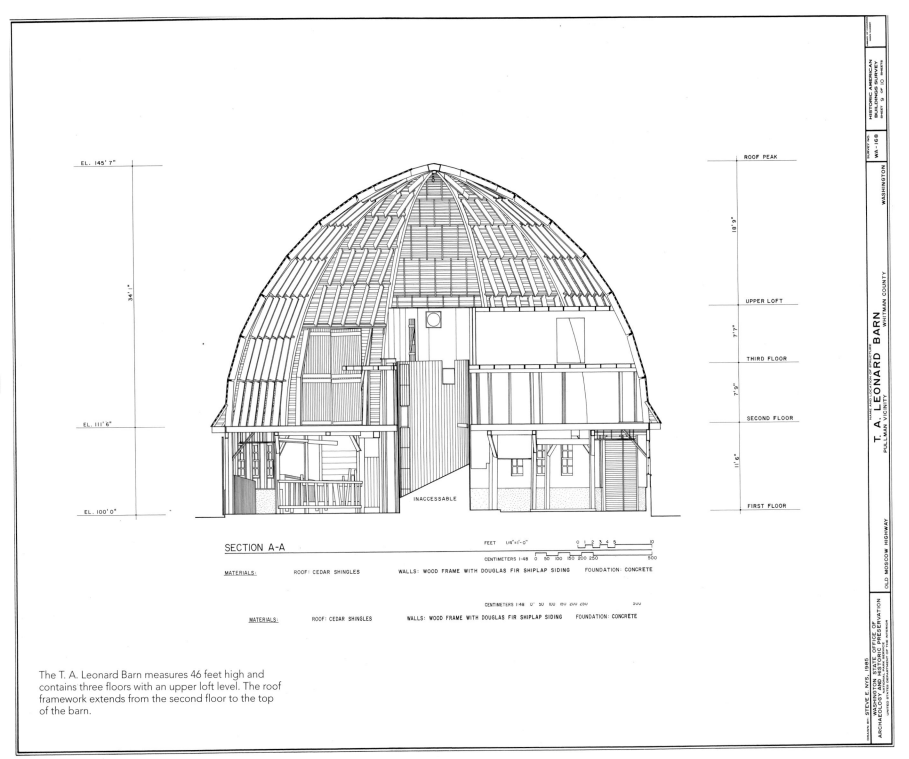

EL. 145' 7"

34' 1"

EL. 111' 6"

EL. 100' 0"

ROOF PEAK

18' 9"

UPPER LOFT

7' 7"

THIRD FLOOR

7' 9"

SECOND FLOOR

11' 6"

FIRST FLOOR

INACCESSIBLE

SECTION A-A

FEET   1/4"=1'-0"

0 1 2 3 4 5   10

CENTIMETERS 1:48   0   50   100   150   200   250   500

MATERIALS: ROOF: CEDAR SHINGLES   WALLS: WOOD FRAME WITH DOUGLAS FIR SHIPLAP SIDING   FOUNDATION: CONCRETE

CENTIMETERS 1:48   0"   50   100   150   200   250   500

MATERIALS: ROOF: CEDAR SHINGLES   WALLS: WOOD FRAME WITH DOUGLAS FIR SHIPLAP SIDING   FOUNDATION: CONCRETE

The T. A. Leonard Barn measures 46 feet high and contains three floors with an upper loft level. The roof framework extends from the second floor to the top of the barn.

DRAWN BY: STEVE E. NYS, 1985

WASHINGTON STATE OFFICE OF
ARCHAEOLOGY AND HISTORIC PRESERVATION
NATIONAL PARK SERVICE
UNITED STATES DEPARTMENT OF THE INTERIOR

NAME AND LOCATION OF STRUCTURE

T. A. LEONARD BARN
PULLMAN VICINITY

OLD MOSCOW HIGHWAY

T. A. LEONARD BARN
WHITMAN COUNTY
WASHINGTON

SURVEY NO.   WA-168

HISTORIC AMERICAN
BUILDINGS SURVEY
SHEET 9 OF 10 SHEETS

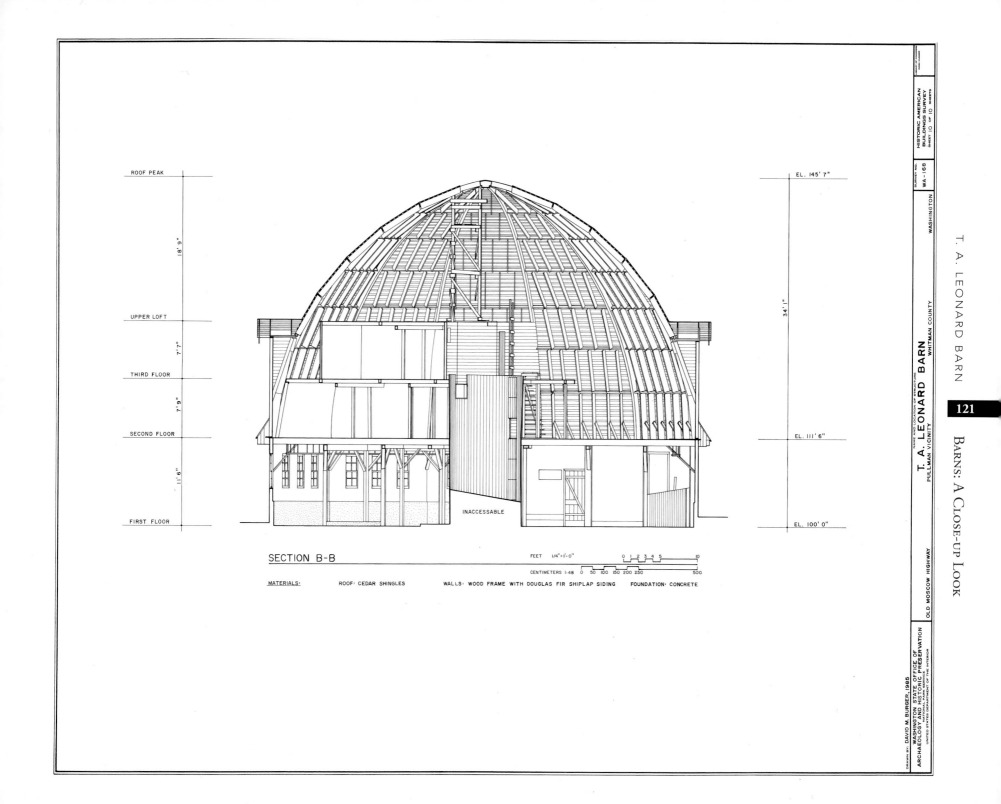

ROOF PEAK

18' 9"

UPPER LOFT

7' 7"

THIRD FLOOR

7' 9"

SECOND FLOOR

11' 6"

FIRST FLOOR

EL. 145' 7"

34' 1"

EL. 111' 6"

EL. 100' 0"

INACCESSABLE

SECTION B-B

FEET   1/4"=1'-0"

CENTIMETERS 1:48

0 1 2 3 4 5   10

0   50 100 150 200 250   500

MATERIALS: ROOF: CEDAR SHINGLES   WALLS: WOOD FRAME WITH DOUGLAS FIR SHIPLAP SIDING   FOUNDATION: CONCRETE

DRAWN BY: DAVID M. BURGER, 1986

WASHINGTON STATE OFFICE OF
ARCHAEOLOGY AND HISTORIC PRESERVATION
NATIONAL PARK SERVICE
UNITED STATES DEPARTMENT OF THE INTERIOR

OLD MOSCOW HIGHWAY

NAME AND LOCATION OF STRUCTURE

T. A. LEONARD BARN
PULLMAN VICINITY   WHITMAN COUNTY

SURVEY NO.
WA-168

HISTORIC AMERICAN
BUILDINGS SURVEY
SHEET 10 OF 10 SHEETS

WASHINGTON

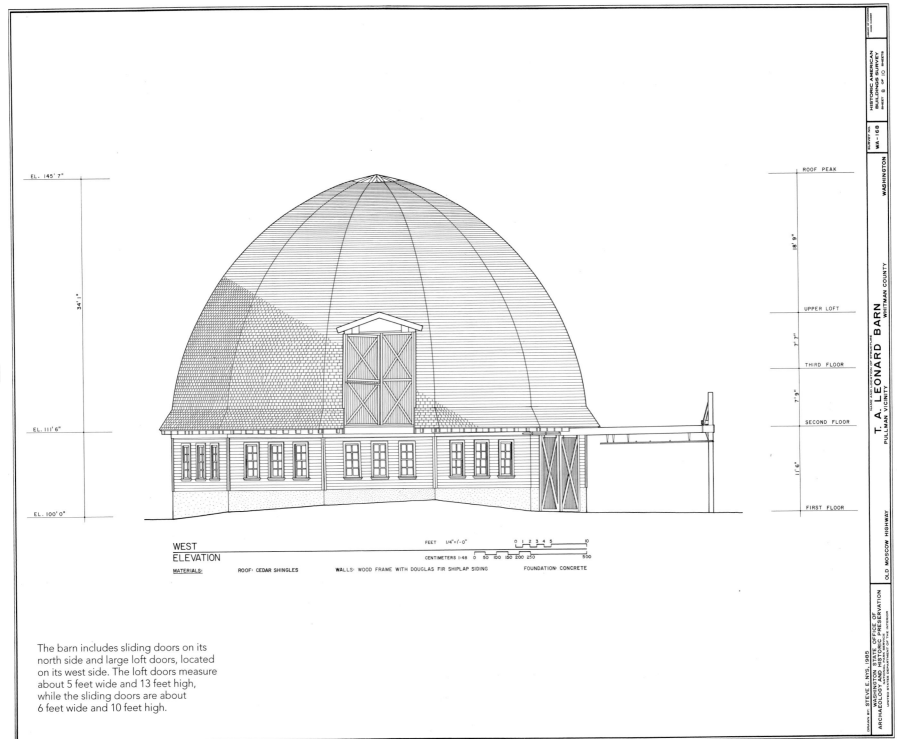

EL. 145' 7"

34' 1"

EL. 111' 6"

EL. 100' 0"

ROOF PEAK

18' 9"

UPPER LOFT

7' 7"

THIRD FLOOR

7' 9"

SECOND FLOOR

11' 6"

FIRST FLOOR

WEST
ELEVATION

FEET   1/4"=1'-0"

0 1 2 3 4 5   10

CENTIMETERS 1:48   0   50   100   150   200   250   500

MATERIALS:

ROOF: CEDAR SHINGLES   WALLS: WOOD FRAME WITH DOUGLAS FIR SHIPLAP SIDING   FOUNDATION: CONCRETE

The barn includes sliding doors on its
north side and large loft doors, located
on its west side. The loft doors measure
about 5 feet wide and 13 feet high,
while the sliding doors are about
6 feet wide and 10 feet high.

DRAWN BY: STEVE E. NYS, 1985

WASHINGTON STATE OFFICE OF
ARCHAEOLOGY AND HISTORIC PRESERVATION
NATIONAL PARK SERVICE
UNITED STATES DEPARTMENT OF THE INTERIOR

SURVEY NO.   WA-168

HISTORIC AMERICAN
BUILDINGS SURVEY
SHEET 8 OF 10 SHEETS

NAME AND LOCATION OF STRUCTURE

T. A. LEONARD BARN
PULLMAN VICINITY   WHITMAN COUNTY   WASHINGTON

OLD MOSCOW HIGHWAY

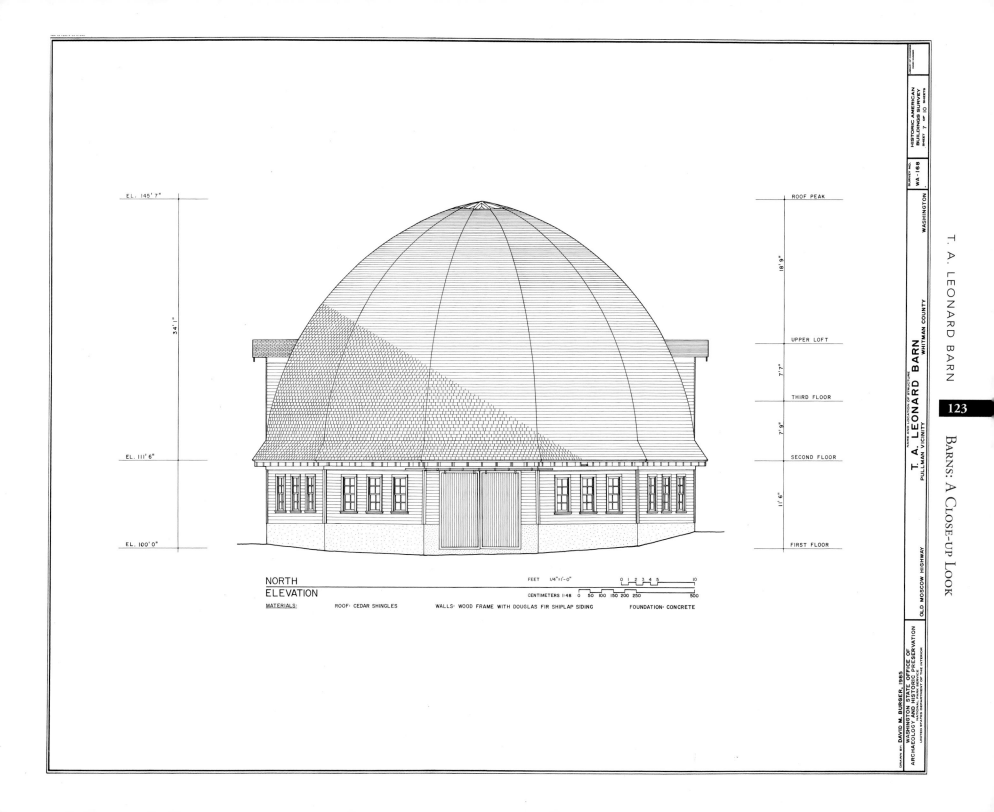

EL. 145' 7" ————— ROOF PEAK

18' 9"

UPPER LOFT

34' 1"

7' 7"

THIRD FLOOR

7' 9"

SECOND FLOOR

EL. 111' 6"

11' 6"

EL. 100' 0" ————— FIRST FLOOR

NORTH
ELEVATION

MATERIALS:

FEET 1/4"=1'-0"

CENTIMETERS 1:48   0   50   100   150 200 250   500

0 1 2 3 4 5   10

ROOF: CEDAR SHINGLES   WALLS: WOOD FRAME WITH DOUGLAS FIR SHIPLAP SIDING   FOUNDATION: CONCRETE

DRAWN BY: DAVID M. BURGER, 1985

WASHINGTON STATE OFFICE OF
ARCHAEOLOGY AND HISTORIC PRESERVATION
NATIONAL PARK SERVICE
UNITED STATES DEPARTMENT OF THE INTERIOR

NAME AND LOCATION OF STRUCTURE
T. A. LEONARD BARN
PULLMAN VICINITY   WHITMAN COUNTY

OLD MOSCOW HIGHWAY

SURVEY NO.
WA-168

HISTORIC AMERICAN
BUILDINGS SURVEY
SHEET 7 OF 10 SHEETS

WASHINGTON

HABS NO. WA-168-1

The roof of the T. A. Leonard barn reaches almost 19 feet above the upper loft floor. A scaffold on the barn's upper level allows access to the interior roof framework.

The barn is built in the shape of a dodecagon, which has twelve sides.

INDEX

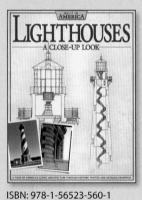

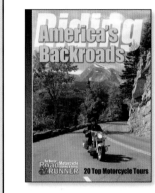

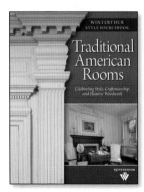
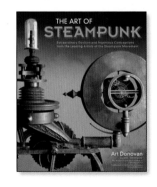